Photographs and Local History

Batsford Local History Series

LOCAL HISTORY:
A HANDBOOK FOR BEGINNERS
Philip Riden

SCOTTISH LOCAL HISTORY:
AN INTRODUCTORY GUIDE
David Moody

RECORD SOURCES FOR LOCAL HISTORY
Philip Riden

CHURCH AND PARISH:
A GUIDE FOR LOCAL HISTORIANS
J. H. Bettey

MAPS FOR LOCAL HISTORY
Brian Paul Hindle

SCOTTISH FAMILY HISTORY
David Moody

FARMING
Peter Edwards

PHOTOGRAPHS AND
LOCAL HISTORY
George Oliver

SOURCES FOR URBAN HISTORY
Stephen Porter

Photographs and Local History

George Oliver

B. T. Batsford Ltd · London

© George Oliver 1989
First published 1989

Typeset by Tameside Filmsetting, Ltd.
and printed in Great Britain by
The Bath Press, Bath

Published by B. T. Batsford Ltd
4 Fitzhardinge Street, London WIH OAH

A CIP catalogue record for this book
is available from the British Library

ISBN 0 7134 5678 7

CONTENTS

Preface 6

1 Photographs as evidence:
    identification and interpretation 8

2 Sources of photographs 34

3 Searching for photographs 64

4 Selection and processing for reproduction 94

5 Photographic techniques for the local historian 117

Bibliography 123

Index 127

PREFACE

Three people are primarily responsible for the fact that I have written this book. The first is Mr William Lind, whose discovery and subsequent purchase of the W. F. Jackson collection was drawn to my attention by the second, Mr Maurice Fleming, who then commissioned me to write about it for *The Scots Magazine*, and the third is Mr David Moody, who had read my articles and suggested to B. T. Batsford that I might be a suitable person to write about the use of old photographs. His own *Scottish Local History*, I may say, set a very high standard to follow.

I thank all three most heartily and I thank my publishers too for allowing me to realise an ambition held since my 'teens, when I first saw and read various volumes in their topographical series on the British Isles and was greatly attracted by excellence of their words, their photographs (and their Brian Cook line drawings) and their typography and design overall. My youthful desire to write and illustrate a Batsford book has been satisfied in full and although severe illness delayed completion of the present work its preparation has been a most pleasant task and one, moreover, made the easier and more enjoyable by the tolerance, sympathy and encouragement of my Editor, Mr Tony Seward.

For obvious reasons few of the photographs were taken by me but all have been gathered during the past forty years or so, my primary interest stimulated by the early contact with Batsford books to which reference has already been made, by work on visual aids material, on mapmaking from aerial photographs during the latter part of the war and on photographic interpretation then and later. Three years in Edinburgh in the early 'fifties, as Art Editor of the old *SMT Magazine*, gave me a grounding in picture research that later work as a transport historian increased and widened in scope. Because of the foresight of Mr Christopher Carrell, Director of Third Eye Centre in Glasgow, I spent more than ten years, from 1975 onward, making a photographic record of all manner of activities there, from exhibition opening ceremonies and installations, through performance art of every possible kind, visits by persons of consequence, prose and poetry readings, dance, mime, theatre and opera workshops, to sponsored outdoor happenings, cafe and bookshop scenes – in fact a day-by-day picture of life in a hyper-active Arts Centre. I have practised, therefore, what I preach here!

I would like to express my deep appreciation of the help that I have received from the following – and to offer my sincere apologies to anyone whose name has been overlooked: The Arnold Library, Arnold, by Nottingham; Lindsay and William Allan, John Annan, Mrs Val Boa, A. J. Browning, Peter Burrin, Christopher Carrell, Mr and Mrs F. Connon, Mrs Lesley Couparwhite, Joe Fisher, Maurice Fleming, J. F. W. Hendry, Brian Lambie, MBE, and the Biggar Museum Trust; Miss Helen Leitch, William Lind, the Local History Forum, Scotland; T. Lochhead, Oscar Marzaroli, Mr and Mrs R. McCracken, Miss Joy Monteith, D. Moody, Michael Moss and the staff of the University of Glasgow Archives; Mark O'Neil and Springburn Museum Trust; Dr L. Paterson and Clyde Shipping Co.; Miss Flora Ritchie, Mrs A. Russell, Alastair Smith and Glasgow Museum of Transport; Messrs Stenson and Harcourt of The Postcard Shop, Glasgow.

The sources of the photographs are as follows: the W. F. Jackson Collection, nos. 4–10, 15, 19, 20, 32–43 (left), 45, 47–50, 65, 87, 103; Clyde Shipping Company, nos. 16, 21–25; Mr and Mrs F. C. Connon, no. 100; Miss Helen Leitch, nos. 88, 89; Mr T. Lochhead, nos. 60, 61; Miss E. Love, no. 62; Mr T. Love, no. 113; Springburn Museum Trust, nos. 30, 51; Mr J. C. Warburg, no. 79. The remainder are from the author's collection.

Finally I would like to express my gratitude to my wife, Cordelia, whose maintained interest, encouragement and advice throughout have been so greatly appreciated.

Chapter One

PHOTOGRAPHS AS EVIDENCE: IDENTIFICATION AND INTERPRETATION

The concern of the local historian is not simply a verbal one. In writing up a project the text will be enhanced if supplemented with pictures, and they are very often essential pieces of evidence. For greatest authenticity and authority such pictures will almost certainly be photographs unless the period to be dealt with is much before 1845. As a primary source of visual information there is nothing better; with remarkably few exceptions the photograph is a generally reliable and truthful witness, alterations to its image being difficult to effect and easy, on the whole, to detect.

Photography is unequalled for the directness of its message, for its special power to transport the viewer to the scene or incident portrayed, for the way in which it can register mood or atmosphere and, above all, for its capacity to provide visual facts in the greatest detail, clarity and number. The accuracy of the photograph is more or less absolute, and in record photography – our principal concern in this book – there is a consistency not always obtained by drawings, where the variable human element takes precedence over the unvarying mechanical one.

For the historian who is examining and analysing photographs, first impressions, however vivid and apparently significant, are never enough. The historian must look and look again, and draw the maximum possible amount of information from the two-dimensional evidence of the photograph, whether in colour, in black and white or in sepia (the single tint most commonly met in elderly prints). He or she must scan every single square centimetre for clues to support or amplify deductions and conclusions already made provisionally. Such stringent tasks cannot be taken to a successful finish without ample knowledge of both the subject in hand and the wider background.

This knowledge need not be of a highly specialised kind. For most of the time, indeed, the proper reading of photographs, almost regardless of age, depends largely on commonsense. Specialised information can then be drawn upon when necessary. This applies as much to the identification of subject matter as it does to the dating of individual photographs. Fortunately the carrying out of the necessary operations tends to be an interesting, sometimes exciting and usually enjoyable affair. There are inevitably 'problem' pictures, however, which baffle, frustrate or annoy.

In some ways the historian is privileged. In the first place, not only does the historian search for and select his or her own illustrations, but he or she is also largely or entirely responsible for deciding which are to be used, should a project go forward to publication. The control that this allows must be exercised with proper restraint, however, and with a constant concern for quality of words as well as of pictures, and for their most effective combination on the page. Secondly, the historian will learn something of the work of the picture researcher – that mixture of the detective and the diplomat, animated by curiosity and unthwartable enthusiasm, supported by patience, perseverance and politeness, and spurred on, always, by the hope that something, some time, of major interest and historic significance is going to turn up.

The present writer is well aware of the special difficulties of finding suitable photographs to complement, and perhaps enhance, a specific text. Aptness of choice of subject matter must have primacy of place at the search and selection stages of picture research, but of comparable importance are sharpness of image and overall quality. This usually means a wide tonal range and a freedom from tears or blemishes. If a photograph under examination is out of focus; is too light or too dark; too flat, tonally speaking, or too 'contrasty'; if it is chemically stained, fogged or faded, or physically damaged, then its potential value as an illustration is diminished. Visual legibility, in every sense, is what a photograph should possess; it matters every bit as much as clear handwriting or the choice of a good typeface where verbal communication is involved. Yet this concern is not always taken as seriously as it ought to be.

The writer is aware also that the local historian in particular must often rely on material borrowed from private sources, with all that this entails in terms of gratitude, and the sense of obligation which may inhibit the adoption of a sufficiently critical attitude. As a general rule, material thus obtained comes from either family albums, which tend to be orderly and captioned (however scantily), or from haphazard collections of loose prints housed in paper wallets or the sturdier sort of shoe box. Such collections usually lack consistency, pictorially speaking, and their technical quality and physical condition will vary from the very good to the very bad (with the majority in the latter category). This applies as much to negatives, where these have survived, as it does to prints. There may be spots, scratches, marks or the occasional fingerprint – and breakages, too, in the case of old glass plates – as well as deterioration of the emulsion and, therefore, the all-important image itself. Such defects, of course, have an adverse effect on pictorial legibility.

If the subject itself is sufficiently interesting and relevant, however, this may not matter. A good example is Fig. 1, showing new Argyll motor cars on horse-drawn carts in Glasgow, early this century, almost certainly on their way from a railway goods yard to a local motor agent's premises (there is, in fact, a delivery note tied to the steering wheel of the foremost vehicle). Its immediate appeal is to the road

1 *New Argyll motor cars en route from factory to showroom, c. 1907.*

transport historian, for whom such rare evidence of one way of moving new cars more than 80 years ago is of special interest. He or she might be inclined to pair it with a photograph of a contemporary, purpose-built car transporter; pictorial comparisons, properly made, can have great visual effect and importance.

There is more to be learned, however, from close and concentrated scrutiny of what, at first sight, seems a somewhat dull and uninteresting picture. Look, for example, at the differences in dress between the formally-suited, bowler-hatted foremen on the one hand and the casually-clothed, cloth-capped carters on the other, their principal sartorial feature a long, protective, leather apron. These differences, incidentally, marked not only their separate work functions but also the social distinction between them, however slight this may have been in practice. It is a matter of record that, cars apart, a similar line-up of Clydesdale horses, carts, carters and their solemn foremen could have been readily arranged 40 years later, so little had these elements changed in the meantime.

Although there is no hard evidence, local knowledge suggests that this photograph was taken in Bell Street, in central Glasgow, around 1907. With specialised knowledge, identification of the Scottish-built cars is made unhesitatingly and a tentative date proposed, simply because the appearance of Argyll cars changed so little between 1906 and 1908. Specialist knowledge also alerted this writer to the fact that the publicity department of Argyll Motors Limited may well have been responsible for the taking of this posed picture, its energetic distribution of press handout photographs to motoring writers and periodicals between 1905 and 1914 (by which time, following a bankruptcy, it had become Argylls Limited) being well known to transport historians.

On the other hand, the photograph might have been taken to the order of Wordie & Company, the Glasgow haulage firm here concerned. Pride in horses and vehicles was strong in the industry and it was no uncommon thing to have a photographic record made, either of a particularly fine turn-out – as at a special parade or local agricultural show, or, as here, of an out-of-the-ordinary load, handled, quite possibly, for the first time.

If rather a lot of attention appears to have been paid to this example it is because it shows how much may be deduced from an apparently straightforward picture. The original, as a matter of interest, was plucked from a pile of discarded paperwork in a long-established garage more than twenty years ago. The place was being demolished before rebuilding; the architect was a friend and, with his interest in the past well known, the writer was invited to rummage and to take away anything of historical importance that he could find. So poor was the condition of this rescued print that it was copied immediately, then properly filed away. Whenever practically and economically possible this routine should be followed as a matter of course. (Yet, more than one picture library still sends out *original* prints to potential users.)

It is always worthwhile to look out for such happenings locally – shops or businesses closing, or premises being pulled down, either for good or to make way for new ones; the demolition of offices, factories, mills, power-stations, hotels, places of entertainment or worship, shipyards, dock or canal buildings, sports grounds and pavilions, town halls and so on. Keep an eye on your local newspaper, tune in to your local radio and listen attentively to local gossip. As soon as you get wind of anything at all to do with your own special historic interests, make immediate contact (if humanly possible) with those most directly involved. A courteous, diplomatic approach to the right person at the right time will greatly increase your chances of obtaining access, sooner or later, to any unwanted documents and photographs that might be left.

There is no point in being shy when such opportunities materialise, or backward in declaring a personal interest. Within reason, the more you disclose at this stage, the greater your chances of being taken seriously and granted preferential treatment. And while it may be thought presumptuous to say so here, do remember to say 'please' and 'thank you' at the appropriate times. The favours, after all, are usually being provided by the other party. Once only in his extensive experience has this writer been refused access to material that was being thrown out, not even his strongest, politest pleas overcoming the determination of the person in the company responsible to burn everything, regardless of its historical value.

At one time there was still the occasional chance of acquiring the contents of a retired or deceased photographer's studio – his carefully filed and documented negative and print files a potential treasure trove for the informed historian. With the widespread interest in old photographs today, however, the possibility of a collection of this kind escaping commercial interests is extremely unlikely. Nevertheless it is always wise to keep ears and eyes open wide for such an eventuality.

It is as well to remind yourself, even at this early stage, that while the search itself may be exciting and enjoyable it is only a means to an end. What is being sought, after all, has to serve specific purposes and unless it can do so there is little point in wasting any more time on it than is absolutely necessary. By all means look at everything that you can lay hands upon, but learn to make quick decisions as to what is, and what is not, worth keeping. Just because a photograph is old and sepia-coloured does not mean that it is good as of right. It has to be looked at as dispassionately as possible, without the intervention of sentiment. When much trouble and time have been taken to gather facts and to make best use of them in verbal form it is of great importance, surely, to spend a comparable amount of time and energy in locating the most appropriate photographs for visual support.

A counsel of perfection? Of course. This is very much easier to advocate than to carry out in practice, but the importance of making the strongest possible efforts to set and sustain high standards must be emphasised. Because so much of the photographic material available is of indifferent quality it is easy to become discouraged, which is where the importance of optimism and perseverance becomes apparent. If you are depressed by your lack of success it sometimes helps to intensify your search. Looking takes time, however, and unless you are cushioned by a generous research grant or sustained by a usefully large publisher's advance (which is unlikely as far as the average local historian is concerned, alas) there is a definite limit to the amount of time to be spared.

In making choices, you have to think in terms of What? Why? Where? Who? When? as a rough and ready starting point. Ask yourself how specific matters may best be illustrated by apt photographs; how items not easily described in words may be most clearly and vividly shown; how the enlightenment of your readers may be most effectively increased by intelligent use of good and suitable pictures, and how their enjoyment of the work in question may be intensified thereby.

Let us now look at some more examples in detail, drawing upon general and specialised knowledge, as and when necessary, for identification, dating and interpretation. Where expert information is unavailable suggestions for finding it are made. We will begin with a picture postcard – the most widely available and usually the least expensive photographic source, with an almost limitless range of subject matter from over the past hundred years.

Our first postcard is unused, which is a pity, as there is no informative postmark on its back to indicate precisely when and where it went into a pillar-box. Because the caption reads 'Main Street, Bangor' and because it is fairly obvious the photograph was taken in the mid-1930s, this might not seem to matter much. In fact, however, there are three Bangors in the British Isles – two in Wales and one in Northern Ireland – and unless one has personal knowledge of two at least there is nothing to be seen here to suggest which of the three it might be.

Or is there? With the aid of the researcher's most immediately useful tool, a good magnifying-glass, let us look, firstly, for distinctive shop or street names to tell us

2 *Main Street, Bangor, from a postcard.*

whether we are in Wales or Ulster. There are no Williams or McGuffies here, however. Common sense and general knowledge having failed, let the author, as a road transport specialist, take over. Looking closely at the visible cars, and then at their registration plates – all of which, apart from that of the Morris 'Eight' saloon on the extreme left, carry the letter 'Z' – the country can be identified as Ireland. Since the introduction of compulsory motor vehicle licensing at the beginning of 1904 use of the letter 'Z' has been restricted to Northern Ireland (and 'I', as a matter of interest, to Eire).

Furthermore, because the Morris 'Eight' did not come onto the market until September 1934 the photograph could not have been taken earlier. Because it is the newest vehicle on the scene the chances are that the picture was made during the following summer. Summer? For one thing, the shop blinds are down, to protect perishable or fadeable goods on show. Further,

the younger pedestrians are wearing warm weather clothing, the men sporting white, open-neck shirts: the women comfortable summer frocks. The fact that most of the older people wear hats and coats is of no seasonal significance; it was the custom then, as it is still to some extent, for mature citizens of both sexes to dress so, in warm weather as well as cold, to conform with the social formalities of being outdoors.

More period details include the aproned butcher's boy, the standardised front of the F. W. Woolworth store (where nothing cost more than 6d – 2½p today) and the general air of order and tidiness. This is a good representative example of a completely unretouched record; here is how Main Street, Bangor looked more than 50 years ago. About the only thing not revealed is the fact that Bangor is a seaside resort.

Our next card does let us know that Bournemouth is, taken as it was from the pier, looking inland towards the beach and the town beyond. It is a populous picture, the approximate dating of which should be handed over to a specialist in period costume (again there is no post-mark to help). Because there is what looks very much like an early motor car on the right, in the background, it is suggested that the date of production was around 1904. On examination, the car seems to have been painted in upon a photograph taken several years earlier. The general air of formality is so marked that Victorian influences, surely, were still prevalent.

One point to remember is that many publishers of postcards sold a particular view for as many years as they could get away with, updating it only when falling sales indicated that it was time to do so. Even then, some publishers were most reluctant to have new negatives made, despite the fact that it was so difficult to paint out existing, out-of-date vehicles and replace them with more modern

ones – which became out-of-date themselves within the year, so rapid was the rate of visual and mechanical change in the road vehicle industry at this early stage in its history. The larger, more visually important, store, shop, cinema, theatre or church, could also be a positive dating feature.

When it comes to landscapes or sea views, however, accurate dating is far less easy – as long as the photographer kept his camera away from the more noticeable kind of man-made feature – prominent public buildings, for instance; major hydro-electric schemes (with their once-controversial pylons); railways, their locomotives and rolling-stock; road vehicles; telegraph poles; four-funnel Atlantic liners, 'Dreadnought' battleships, paddle pleasure-steamers and so on. As long as these were kept out of sight the landscape or seascape card would have had a long and profitable selling life.

To some extent formality is a feature of the fine photograph of Ostend beach, taken in 1908 by W. F. Jackson (Fig. 4). (As an amateur, he had no need to exercise what was, in effect, a

3 *Bournemouth, from a contemporary postcard, c. 1904.*

Bournemouth. From the Pier looking South. 3675.

4 *Ostend beach in high summer, 1908.*

sort of visual censorship, so here nothing is left out.) Notable features here are the quality of the light – the gentle, twinkling sunshine that accurate exposure has captured so successfully – and the great amount of information that a really careful choice of viewpoint and a steady hold on the camera provide. The children building sandcastles do so with their hats on (it is high summer after all). The men are dressed in black, in the main; not too many of the women wear white. The distinctively shaped cane or wicker beach-chairs and the wheeled bathing-machines (the latter drawn well back from the chill North Sea) give the scene much of its period flavour, along with the fluttering flags that are of considerable visual interest.

In this connection, consider how important a

place smoke or steam once had in photographs of towns and docks, giving life to what otherwise might have been lacklustre scenes. One photographer especially skilled in this respect is Andreas Feininger, whose books, *Feininger's Chicago, 1941* and *New York in the Forties* include many views animated by smoke, by steam, by mist or by clouds, as well as by crowds of people. Another outstanding photographer of the urban scene, Berenice Abbott, made equally effective use of these elements in many of the pictures in her book *New York in the Thirties*. In all these works documentary photography is seen at a very high level. (For publication details, see Bibliography, p. oo.)

Fig. 1.4 is an example of the kind of photograph which should be used at as large a size as possible, as it is so rich in information and so attractive in its mix of facts and atmosphere that it compels attention. It would serve well as the 'establishing shot' in a sequence of seaside pictures, for example, for a book or for a magazine article, supported by close-up photographs of individual, related subjects – holidaymakers themselves, singly or in groups; deck-chairs and bathing-machines, along with their occupants and attendants; builders of sandcastles, bathers, paddlers, riders of donkeys and rowers of boats; fishers with rods, nets, or string and bent pin; beach entertainers, religious gatherings, large- or small-scale picnics and organised sports.

To a limited extent W. F. Jackson did photograph subjects of this kind, but most of his seaside activities were centred on the recording of his immediate family, close relatives and friends, sunny summer after sunny summer, until 1914. In August 1912 he made a 5 in × 4 in 13cm × 10cm) negative of a family picnic on Gullane beach that is of especially high pictorial and technical quality (Fig. 5). Posed it most certainly was – but with such skill that it has the look of the kind of 'candid' photograph to which

we are so well accustomed nowadays. But there was no question of a 'grab shot' at a time when the sort of apparatus used was large and noticeable, properly manageable only when perched high on a tripod.

In this case, however, the sitters are as well composed as the picture itself. Such is the sharpness overall that we get an exceptional chance to study the minutiae of a middle-class picnic: one where the formality of dress is in strong contrast to the eating and drinking arrangements, which are of a totally informal sort. The sandwiches were carried in a much-used McVittie & Price biscuit tin and a limited choice of drinks was provided from a pair of Thermos flasks and a couple of bottles of some kind of 'Sparkling beverage'. The tilted tin of Bourneville cocoa probably held sugar; its label design, incidentally, did not change for another 40 years or so. As for the clothes, we see with greatest clarity the high quality of their design and fabrication, and of the materials used. We are able to contrast the general simplicity of the skirts, dresses and blouses with the elaboration of the headgear.

By the time Cadbury changed their cocoa label the heyday of beach entertainment was

5 *Picnic on a Scottish seashore, 1912.*

6 *The Pierrots' Show, which took place by the sea – as here – or on the pier, was once a main attraction at many resorts.*

past. But when Jackson came upon the scene in North Berwick, in 1911, Erick's Entertainers – all four in traditional pierrot's dress – had attracted a reasonably large audience (Fig. 6). Much of the appeal of this photograph lies in the fact that it shows a once-familiar public activity.

No doubt the Jacksons, their relatives and friends patronised Erick's on suitable summer days when not otherwise engaged – as, for example, in taking formal afternoon tea in the garden of 'Faussethill', their Gullane residence that year (Fig. 7). The garden seat and a pair of deck-chairs have been joined by two tables and a decorated cake-stand from indoors, and the presence of a number of newly bound books inclines one to suppose that culture may well have been a part of the feast. These finely dressed females must, surely, have been celebrating a special occasion. For once, all hats are off (perhaps to show how carefully and attractively each individual's hair has been arranged?); fine china is to hand, decorative doyleys billow round the plates of bread and French cakes, and the teapot and hot water pot

7 *Another highly formalised ceremony (held only in the summer, for obvious reasons) was the taking of tea in the garden.*

shelter below lace-topped cosies.

Several times a year until 1914 the Jacksons and two of their nieces, along with at least one camera, went off on holidays in Scotland, England and the Continent, one important consequence of which was a regular addition to the number of pictures in the family albums. In November 1913 the Jacksons were in Windsor and from a window of the White Hart Hotel the memorable shot of the castle (Fig. 8) was taken.

Its special quality of light and atmosphere, combined with the presence of so much detailed information, particularly distinguish it. Less than a year later, Jackson caught a couple of golfers strolling towards a train at Gullane station. At Rothesay, a Clyde estuary resort, Jackson came across the horse-drawn newsagent's van shown in Fig. 10 one day in 1928. It has stopped raining and the driver/salesman has stepped out to serve a customer. A good partner for this picture would be a photograph of a typical seaside newsagent's shop today: static, its outside alive with balloons, beach balls, buckets and spades, fluttering, noisy celluloid windmills on sticks,

8 (above) *This is more than just a record photograph. Because of the time it was taken – in the early morning after the rain – it is strongly atmospheric in mood.*

9 (left) *Gullane Station after the start of the First World War, when there were still three classes of passenger accommodation on trains.*

10 (opposite) *Although the newspaper vendor is still an everyday sight, vans of this type – which were never common – have now disappeared completely.*

and selections of view and comic postcards.

Photographs such as those discussed above have various practical uses – as illustrations for a seaside feature in book or article form; for a study of shop types, both static and mobile, or for an examination of the practical uses of the horse-drawn vehicle. For the latter the picture of the Argyll cars perched high on their carts (Fig. 1) would be appropriate, as would the early twentieth-century laundry van in Fig. 11 that looks as if it has just arrived outside its

owner's premises, brand new and gleaming. Its white bags and cane baskets, of varying sizes, were in general use until the 1940s, at least, and the close attention paid to lettering and decoration was typical of this and many other trades, for which a smart, well turned-out vehicle was an effective and economical mobile advertisement.

Until the early 1950s the sight and sound of trace-horses helping heavily laden carts up the long slope of West Nile Street, in the centre of Glasgow, was so familiar that few passers-by took conscious heed (Fig. 12). The same was true for most other everyday happenings and it was their very 'ordinariness' that caused the majority of photographers to ignore them. Only

---

11 *The design and appearance of horse-drawn vehicles reached heights of excellence which were not equalled by the motor car for a very long time.*

12 *Wordie & Co., whose carts appear in Fig. 1, were still active in 1948, as the lettering on the tailboard of this cart shows.*

---

a few, far-sighted individuals realised that much of what was to be seen on a daily basis would soon disappear, and did what they could to make a record that would be of great value at a later date. It is not until one is searching for pictures of this sort that one begins to realise how rare they are. Growing awareness should lead one to think about laying down, as it were, a personal collection now; one covering in as great detail and scope as possible one's personal, historical interests with good, sharp pictures that could be used at a later time as illustrations for work projects. The fact that

your local greengrocer letters specimen prices of fruit and vegetables on the insides of his windows every working day of the year may appear to be of little interest at the moment – but imagine how factually and visually valuable it might be in the future, showing an everyday working practice of our time, as well as the cost of specific products at a particular time in history. Details of subject, place, time of day and date, person or persons and any special reason for taking the photograph should be recorded.

Since the end of the Second World War an increasing interest in the preservation and use of horse-drawn vehicles has been bringing them to more general attention, especially at agricultural or horse shows where we may see them in motion and very much alive, rather than stationary and to all intents and purposes dead, in museums. The style and elegance of form of a well-turned out horse-drawn vehicle, for instance, may be well seen in Fig. 13, taken outside the Richmond showground.

Traditionally, gypsies, showmen and canal bargees, and their families, have cherished their specially decorated vans and vessels, once so familiar a sight in many parts of the country but seldom encountered nowadays. Probably the best chance of seeing the traditional types of caravan is at one of the fairly numerous horse fairs still held around the country, and although our once great canals have been reduced almost to nothing in terms of commercial activity, a revival of interest in some of them, at least, as places for pleasure and relaxation now provides opportunities for seeing something of their former glories (Fig. 14).

Perhaps, however, the special quality of the waterways of the past has gone completely. Its distinction was as strong as that of the railways before steam power was replaced by the impersonal diesel or electric locomotive. In each case there was an instantly recognisable, closed-off, private working world, with its own special modes of living and its own unique commercial and industrial architecture.

As a top official of one of the two most important Scottish railway companies, W. F. Jackson had a professional interest in railways that is reflected in many of his photographs. It must be said, nonetheless, that these are by no

13 *Elegance of form and subtlety of proportion were not exclusive to the horse-drawn carriage. They were also shared by more workaday vehicles.*

14 *Like gypsies and showmen, canal bargees were greatly interested in the decoration of their craft – a mixture of stylish realism, as in the case of the painted castles and roses, and geometric patterning.*

means his best, on the whole, and that their number, surprisingly, is not large. When the present writer first saw the photograph reproduced as Fig. 15 he knew nothing about the person who had taken it; indeed, available evidence at the time suggested that he might have been a churchman of some importance, so numerous were the accompanying portraits of ministers of religion, their large families and their substantial Scottish manses. A guess was made that this was a special train, for engineers concerned with line inspection duties, perhaps. When, at a much later date, information was received from the other side of the world that the photographer was W. F. Jackson, and that he was a senior executive of the North British Railway Company, the true nature of the tiny train was realised. Indeed, it was a 'special' – but a special for the use of the General Manager. Here was a case of a working knowledge being insufficient to solve a simple problem of subject identification. In the event, had information not been forthcoming the advice of experts in the subject would have been sought. (Model railways clubs are a particularly good source of information; the amount of knowledge shared by members is often staggering, and is usually willingly passed on to any interested non-member.)

Our next example (Fig. 16) comes from an entirely different source and time; indeed, it may well have been taken more than a century ago. The original from which it was copied is a $3\frac{1}{4}$ in (8cm) square glass lantern-slide, a black and white of first-class tonal quality and exemplary sharpness. Until comparatively recently, the making of monochrome slides of this size and kind was taken most seriously by amateurs and professionals alike, and exceptionally high standards were reached. Look out for boxes of them at sales; there are still plenty about if you look long enough and hard enough, and because of their combination of large size and extreme crispness of image (as a rule) they are in no way difficult to copy onto black and white or colour film.

From the name 'Plymouth' painted on fish-boxes in Fig. 16, we can deduce that the photograph was taken somewhere in the harbour of that notable naval port. In due course a print might be sent to the City Librarian there for positive identification; in the meantime the picture may be savoured for its own sake. Under close scrutiny with a good glass it gives one a vivid sense of being present, of being on the very edge of a scene once commonplace but now, of course, totally unfamiliar. To a lesser degree, the same might be said of Fig. 17, the traction engines hauling a new locomotive from the North British Locomotive works in Springburn, Glasgow, to the docks, for export a year or two after the end of the Second World War. This was a regular sight in Glasgow until the mid-1950s.

Both Fig. 16 and Fig. 17 have pictorial impact; each has a period look that attracts immediate interest; in consequence each is suitable for cover use on a book or booklet, or as a lead picture in a magazine article. Their tonal strength is also important; they can be seen and 'read' from a distance, a primary concern for a front cover illustration.

A photograph as charged with facts as that of Salisbury Market (Fig. 18) is best reproduced at medium to large size. Where so much information is crowded onto the negative it is only fair that it should be made properly visible. This might involve judicious cropping. One of the benefits of handling many photographs is that in the process of weeding out the most suitable you gradually become better at it – and quicker, too. Some lucky people are born with 'an eye for a picture' whether they become photographers or picture editors or not. Others have to learn from scratch the differences between an ordinary and an exceptional picture; one way is to look at what is used by others and to ask yourself why.

Figs. 19 and 20 are examples of good and not-so-good photographs. The occasion was a Sunday School outing to Niddrie, Edinburgh,

---

15 *A Managing Director's Special, east of Aberdour, in Fife, Scotland, 1914. Its solitary passenger was behind the camera when this photograph was taken.*

16 There is a majestic quality about this Plymouth harbour scene which raises it far above the average. The tall bowler hats might help the expert to guess at an approximate date.

17 *Such a sight we will never see: the slow progress of this all-steam procession has caused a great build-up of tramcars behind it.*

on 6 June 1914. W. F. Jackson took his establishing shot (Fig. 19) first of all, with everyone lined up, square to the camera, with dutiful smiles on most faces and no one with closed eyes. It is fine as a record photograph but visually dull. Jackson then continued to take pictures while the distribution of sandwiches and tea took place. The best of these is reproduced as Fig. 20, which gives the viewer a very strong feeling of being there, of being noticed by some present (the ones already served, it will be noticed!) and utterly ignored by others. The composition is excellent. There

is no feeling at all that this picture was prearranged; it has life; it is a snatch of social history – note, for instance, that the teachers stand aloof in the background, like officers dutifully present at an other ranks' party.

The Sunday School set is a specimen of its kind. Another is the sequence of land and sea subjects (Figs. 21–25), made from large ($3\frac{1}{4}$ in. square) lantern-slides owned by the Clyde Shipping Company of Glasgow (reproduced here by special permission). It is known that those taken aboard ship were commissioned for use in company publicity material at a time when a sailing between Glasgow and Cork was an important feature of its programme. When exactly they were taken, no one knows, but the fact that they shared a box with slides of Irish scenes dated 1909 is enough to indicate a

56   SALISBURY

18 (left above) *The open-air market at Salisbury, early this century. Although much is happening there is a strong sense of order. Notice the auction ring for sheep and the long row of chicken coops running diagonally across the picture.*

19 (left below) *The taking of large group photographs is not easy. Persuading everyone to look at you, look cheerful and keep their eyes open can present major problems. This group portrait is of a Sunday School outing.*

20 (below) *The same place and occasion as Fig. 19, but a far more expressive photograph, charged with life and atmosphere.*

possible year. Circumstantial evidence may not be entirely trustworthy, but it can be of real value in suggesting starting points for further research.

How would one go about further research in this particular case? To begin with, the Clyde Shipping Company records are now held in the University of Glasgow archives, where they are readily accessible. Obviously they would be consulted. Then a selective study could be made of the shipping columns and classified advertisement columns of the *Glasgow Herald* newspaper at intervals between, say, 1905 and 1910. Finally, letters asking if any reader remembers the photographs being taken could be written to the editors of the *Herald* or other local newspapers. This would involve a good deal of work, and might not produce much in

21 *SS* Coningbeg, *one of the Clyde Shipping Company's fleet of passenger and cargo-carrying steamers, pictured early this century.*

the way of new facts. On the other hand, someone might come up with material of real value and interest – memories of the service, perhaps; or even better photographs. This happens on occasion, after the publication of letters asking for readers' help maybe, or of a relevant article. Anyone who has ever contributed to the *Scots Magazine* will vouch for its special power to attract 'feedback' from readers all over the world.

It is possible that the Irish pictures, along with many others, were shown by 'magic lantern' to prospective passengers in churches and womens' guilds, at literary and dramatic societies or at clubs of various sorts. The sailings, by the way, were two-day affairs. The steamer travelled out one day to Cork, where its passengers stayed overnight and the next morning visited such places of interest in the neighbourhood as the Blarney Stone, before returning to Glasgow.

The value of now-obsolete glass lantern slides is considerable. At best their qualities of sharpness and rich tonal range, along with well-seen subject matter, make them highly suitable for conversion to black and white prints. Do not overlook them in your searching; they still turn up for sale, or they may be hidden away and forgotten, as was the case with the Clyde Shipping archive that Dr L. Paterson discovered and is now using to proper effect.

22 *Aboard ship,* en route *for Cork, cheerful children pose on deck.*

As a matter of interest this size and type of slide did not go entirely out of use until it was finally ousted by 35mm colour transparencies during the nineteen-fifties. Much interesting and useful material in the larger format has survived from the between-wars period when, incidentally, the craft of making first-class lantern slides was still quite widely practised.

23 (left above) *Passengers relaxing during the Clyde Shipping Company's Glasgow–Cork sailing*, c. *1908.*

24 (left below) *The caption on the slide from which this photograph is taken reads 'Deck Billiards' but this is surely a game of draughts played on a large scale.*

25 (above) *Transport on land was provided for Clyde Shipping passengers by Irish jaunting cars, a line of which are about to depart for Blarney Castle in this photograph*, c. *1908.*

Chapter Two
SOURCES OF PHOTOGRAPHS

In his introduction to the catalogue of the Second World Exhibition of Photography, 1968, the organiser, Dr Karl Pawek, wrote that 1800 million photographs are taken every year. Whatever his authority for it, this figure does give some idea of the magnitude of photographic activity in modern times. It indicates, moreover, that in any attempt to estimate the total number of photographs taken since the 1840s we would have to think in terms of billions.

Of course, enormous numbers of these photographs have vanished, for one reason or another, and of the many millions left the majority have little more than personal and sentimental associations to recommend them – not that these are without value to the historian on occasion. Broadly speaking, however, our concern is not with such pictures, but with those more closely connected to our own

26 *It is difficult to guess what form of summer outing is pictured in this photograph, but both children and adults are wearing their best clothes, and there is a donkey present. The postmark on the card reads 'Darwen 1904'. Sunnyhurst, it would appear, is in Lancashire.*

particular area of study. As local historians, whatever our interest, we work within quite narrow boundaries, geographically speaking, and the relatively modest scale of our enterprises means that the task of finding a few photographs from so many usually turns out to be a little less difficult than expected. It is seldom easy, however, unless one is lucky, and it is satisfying only when enough of the sought-after material is finally tracked down.

For the time being let us concentrate on 'official' sources. These are generally accessible to us all, and increase in number, scope and importance every year. To begin with, we need go no further than the nearest library. These days, more likely than not, it will have a local history section which, if experience is anything to go by, will be in the care of a keen and well-informed member of staff. Almost certainly, there will be a collection of photographs of local interest – the usual starting point for local historical picture research. With good fortune one may find the desired material on the spot, but it is more probable that one will only find a certain amount locally and have to look further afield for more.

Already, help will have been solicited in your library: you will have established contact with its resident expert (who may well become a friend in time and who will tell you of other local sources, both public and private, elsewhere in the country). He or she may ask if you are a member of any of the 'learned' societies in the neighbourhood – concerned with architecture, archaeology, botany, conservation, industrial archaeology, local history, railways, waterways and so on – and if you have been in touch with their respective secretaries to spread awareness of whatever project you happen to be engaged on. At all times, it is important to let as many people as possible know what you are doing – though there may be good reasons, occasionally, for keeping your research to yourself.

There may be a local history museum in your vicinity, in which case you are fortunate. Apart from the collection of photographs of local interest that is an important feature of such places nowadays there will be exhibits that may

well serve as subjects for illustrations. As it is standard practice to have a photographic record of these on file, your range of choice is increased considerably. In some museums (the Victoria and Albert, in London, for example) it is possible to photograph exhibits by previous arrangement; indeed it is even possible to hire studio space at the V. and A. for a moderate fee.

In addition, there is a growing number of museums that show certain large items out of doors. Beamish, south of Newcastle, is one, with a row of furnished cottages, an 1867 station, locomotives and other railway exhibits, a farmstead, a colliery and tramcars. The Ironbridge Gorge Museum in Shropshire is another, where you may see the oldest iron bridge in the world, a blast furnace and steam-blowing machines, pit heads, a printing shop and a canal inclined-plane. The number of transport museums increases slowly; items of road, rail, sea and air are represented at different scales and displayed in different ways; vehicles, vessels and flying machines on show are backed-up by photographs, literature, components, accessories, etc. Apart from the richness of its vehicle collection, the National Motor Museum at Beaulieu, Hampshire, also has a first-class library of transport literature and photographs – and a quick and efficient service, moreover, for the researcher.

A main reason for drawing attention to places where there are large exhibits is to make the point that when it is possible to walk round, say, an early cottage, this gives one a much more satisfying experience than peering at a model, however good, through the glass of an airtight display case.

It has already been pointed out that you may have to search outside your own neighbourhood for material. Like many other things, photographs can finish up a long way from home, a fact that applies for the most obvious of reasons to picture postcards – one good excuse for looking closely wherever and whenever you come across them. Work from the leading British postcard publishers (Frith, Tuck, Valentine and Washington Wilson) is to be found in public and private collections all over

Great Britain. If you come across a really serious collector near you, make contact as soon as possible and make friends if you can, for he or she could become a significant help. As a matter of interest, Birmingham has something like 180,000 items in its Central Library History and Geography Department's topographical postcard collection.

To discover what is available in this country is easy as long as you can lay hands on a copy of *Picture Sources, UK*. If you are unsuccessful locally, make use of the excellent inter-library loan scheme. The above-mentioned publication is large and expensive, but a quite unique record of what there is in public collections, whether large or small, and in the numerous commercial picture libraries that exist to serve the needs of publishers and their authors, as well as historians, illustrators, film, theatre and television picture researchers, advertising agencies and design studios.

The number of items and the range of choice is truly enormous. The Hulton Picture Company lists over 9 million items, Popperfoto 3 million, and the Mansell Collection around 2 million. In the Central Office of Information files there are 250,000 pictures taken between 1920 and the present. (It is worth noting that this Government Information Service runs its photographic side along commercial lines.) Aerofilms, involved in aerial photography since 1919, has about 800,000 subjects; Edwin Smith Photographs a tenth of that number, taken between 1935 and 1971; the National Trust has 23,000 from the 1890s to date, and the National Trust for Scotland 40,000, covering much the same period. The Northern Ireland Information Service offers 2000 photographs of life in Ulster – and makes no charge for their reproduction, which is rare.

An important feature of Aberdeen University Library is its splendid 40,000-strong collection of prints and glass negatives made by, or under the direction of, George Washington Wilson between 1860 and 1900, covering not only Scotland and England but Gibraltar and the Mediterranean, as well as South Africa and Australia. The Public Record Office in Belfast

has 100,000 items, from 1850 to the present day; the University College of North Wales has around 1500, illustrating the local history of that region since 1870, while Aberystwyth Public Library has a total of 15,000 items from 1860 to date. The latter is another source of free photographs: no charge is made for reproduction, and the subject matter of its collection includes rural life, farming, local industries such as lead mining and shipbuilding, maritime activities, transport, commerce and architecture.

The 1200 photographs in the library at Arnold, near Nottingham, date from 1870; unusually, there are a number of vertical and oblique aerial views of the town. The collection of some 5000 photographs in the Abington Museum is concerned with Northamptonshire local and social history. Apart from public houses from 1890 to 1910 it contains pictures of towns and villages and their inhabitants taken between 1890 and 1920.

University libraries and archives are sometimes overlooked, perhaps because we tend to think of them as custodians of words alone. Two have been mentioned so far, but two more can be singled out for attention because of the items of special interest that they contain. Reading University has many photographs of the university itself, along with pictures of the Astor family, agricultural subjects in its Museum of English Rural Life and the Huntley and Palmer's biscuit factory, amounting in all to about 2000 separate items. The very much larger, highly specialised collection at the

27 (right above) *An oblique aerial view that relates its main subject – the St Rollox Railway Works at Springburn, Glasgow – to its surroundings.*

28 (right below) *An excellent low-level oblique view – but of what? A pencilled note on the back of the print suggests that the buildings are somewhere in Dundee, in which case we might be looking at one of the jute mills so numerous there between the wars. The surrounding houses do not look Scottish, however . . .*

University of Cambridge, with 350,000 items, contains aerial photographs of architectural, archaeological, ecological and geographical interest.

In general, the oblique, low-level aerial photograph is the one most useful to the historian. Because of the extremely high quality of the equipment used and the great skills of its operators, clarity and sharpness are characteristic features. As well as showing its main subject, a well-taken oblique relates this to its surroundings in a way almost impossible from ground level. The view of St Rollox Railway Works (Fig. 27) makes this point most effectively; moreover, it is easily comprehended by the layman, for whom the vertical aerial photograph means little or nothing. It may be possible, on rare occasions, for comparative purposes, to pair a vertical view with a map of the area it covers. Remember, however, that this kind of photograph has to be reproduced on as large a scale as possible, otherwise most of its detail will be lost.

The term 'low-level' is comparative, of course; as far as built-up areas go this will be 1000 ft (305m) at least, because of flying rules and regulations. If the oblique is taken from a mountain or a hill-top it may be much higher or much lower; if taken from a tall building, lower still. Before the fashion for tower blocks afflicted this country the photographer tended to think in terms of church steeples if he or she lived in the country, and of high office buildings or other suitable vantage points if a city-dweller.

Local directories are primary sources for many different projects, and also provide much basic material to assist in dating. They are usually accurate to within a year or two, which is more than can be said for maps, enormously useful as these undoubtedly are. Maps, nonetheless, may be vital for determining rough dating and identification and the larger the scale the greater the factual information they carry. The sheets of the early one-inch series that are now out of copyright are now being reprinted and sold at very reasonable prices.

Another source that tends to be overlooked is old documentary films. The best place to see these nowadays (unless there is a film archive in your area) is on television, either on their own or as part of a modern production dealing with a specific historical subject. To make a regular study is to greatly enlarge one's knowledge and understanding of earlier times and, in particular, to increase personal awareness of the fact that, while the look of things and places can change very considerably, human activities and behaviour do not, to anything like the same extent. The top-hatted gentleman leaping on to the platform of a horse-drawn bus has his modern counterpart – hatless and informally dressed, no doubt, but obliged to go through the same kinds of physical motions. Probably, the film image has greater credibility for us because of its apparent life; because the people that it shows us actually move it is much easier to relate to them as living beings like ourselves. At one time this was not quite so easy; silent film stock projected at sound-film speeds generated a jerkiness of movement that was decidedly strange and unreal. A further problem was the harsh contrast, poor image quality and relative lack of sharpness of the nitrate-base film in use. By the 1920s however, that had been resolved in full. It is possible to make frame enlargements from black and white movie film, and this is yet another source to keep in mind. The best results will be obtained from 35mm originals; the worst, by far, from 8 or 9.5mm.

Something of the feeling of 'being there' is to be gained from close scrutiny of sizeable photographs of above-average quality – for example, almost any of the Frith views of British cities, towns and villages taken around the turn of the century. By the time the latter were made, the dry-collodion plate enabled higher shutter speeds to be used, and this, in turn, allowed the photographer to take street scenes containing people and moving traffic. Examining earlier photographs can be a rather eery experience – a totally depopulated street being somewhat outside our experience.

Information on sources of all kinds is to be found in *Picture Sources, UK*. Another most useful work of reference is the *Picture*

Researcher's Handbook, which also lists overseas sources. Neither of these first-rate books is cheap; however, a modestly priced annual, *Museums and Art Galleries in Great Britain and Ireland*, has been on the market for a number of years, and its carefully arranged contents make reference a rapid and enjoyable matter. There are 'Subject' and 'Geographical' indexes and an alphabetical list of museums and art galleries.

Although the first two publications mentioned above indicate the kinds of charges made by the organisations that they list, they do not give actual figures, which, perhaps, is understandable in inflationary times. This makes it difficult for the local historian to arrive at a budget for illustrations. Like it or not, this can cause problems: reproduction fees often reach remarkably high levels – unreasonable ones, sometimes, in this writer's opinion. In general, picture libraries base their charges on the kind of use that photographs from their files are put to. For instance a picture for reproduction on many millions of lager cans will attract a very much higher fee than one for use in a parish magazine. On the whole, rates determined by the kind and scale of use are logical. When you are discussing them, make much of the fact that *your* publication is unlikely to sell in great numbers (however much you hope it will) and that your budget for illustrations is tiny.

Naturally you will take and use free material whenever you are able. Apart from the few libraries and museums that allow reproduction of their photographs without fees (but, quite properly, make a charge for search time, prints, postage, etc.) the other principal free sources are within commerce and industry. Even here, though, some payment may be asked for.

A practical problem lies in the fact that so many organisations have concentrated their administrative activites in one place in recent years, largely because of ever-rising overheads. London is favoured, more often than not, which can make access somewhat difficult, as well as time-consuming and costly. Moreover, this reduces one's chances of making one's own selection of prints from a collection; for obvious reasons this is always better than relying on someone elsewhere to do it for you. And yet – in the writer's experience – where the latter course has to be followed, for some good practical reason, he has seldom been disappointed. It is essential in this case to know exactly what you are looking for, and to describe it in as much detail as you possibly can, with relevant information on your project in précis form.

Where the organisation that you think can help you is local, or has a local office, your first approach should always be to the Publicity Officer, Public Relations Officer or Manager. You may already know who this is; if not, telephone the company concerned before you write. This is good manners, for one thing; for another it is good public relations on your part, indicating a seriousness of intent and a professionalism of attitude that may be favourably noted.

If the organisation is located outside your local area, follow the same procedure, unless the cost of telephoning is too much for your working budget, in which case you write. However you make the initial approach, remember to explain the *aims* of your project and the kind of photographs you seek for it with brevity, clarity and accuracy. Busy people, whoever and wherever they may be, are not going to waste valuable time trying to make sense of a badly presented, rambling and largely illegible letter. Type it, if at all possible, or ask a friend who works in an office to do it for you. Always offer to meet any reasonable charges that may be incurred, and always enclose a stamped, addressed envelope when you write. This makes a good impression immediately – and practically guarantees a reply.

Now, let us assume that you are preparing a short survey of the development of domestic heating and lighting in your county between 1900 and 1940. With the help of a library or museum local history specialist, you have already assembled a number of good photographs of interiors (see Fig. 29) but lack pictures of individual appliances. You have been told of a distant museum that has a specialist collection of photographs of domestic

furniture and household equipment, and have written to its Director to ask what subject matter is available and how much it is going to cost to make use of it. You will also have been in touch with the surviving local coal merchant and with the Gas and Electricity Board showrooms to ask if there is anything of interest still in their possession, or known to them.

Needless to say, your family and friends have been told about your search – but nothing has turned up so far, either from them or from the other sources already approached. In casual conversation at work, however, someone tells you that a large firm that made much domestic cooking equipment before the war has been in the financial news recently. Because its name sounds familiar you examine the photographs in your possession and, after close scrutiny with a magnifying-glass, discover the name and location of the company in question on several coal-fired ranges, dating from 1905 to 1924. It happens that there is a large reference library in your town, with a complete set of British telephone directories, and after five minutes of looking through the appropriate volume you come away knowing that the company is still in existence at its original address. Because this is somewhat distant you decide to write in the first instance, directing your letter to the Public Relations Department, outlining the reasons for your approach, describing the kind of subject matter and photographs you seek, clearly and accurately, offering to meet any costs due and enclosing a stamped, addressed envelope.

You are in luck! The company is proud of its history, flattered, it appears, by your interest, and most anxious to help. It has a collection of old photographs, catalogues, illustrated sales literature, instruction leaflets and books, etc., and to give you a sample of what is available sends you a number of photocopies of various items. In reply you specify half a dozen

different subjects that would cover your needs; in due course they arrive and with them a note to let you know that there is no charge. Your letter of acknowledgement and thanks is cordial, to say the least.

Neither the Gas nor the Electricity Board is able to help with pictures. However, the coal merchant suggests that you try the local builders' merchant, a long established family business well known throughout the county. Once again you are in luck; the founder's family are still in control, the directors are historically-minded and much old material has been preserved. This you discover during your first telephone call, when you speak to whoever is responsible for the company archives.

You arrange an early appointment. A run of electrical appliance and lighting catalogues, along with price lists from 1905 to 1914, has survived, a feature of which is their large and well reproduced illustrations (see Fig. 30). You are offered photocopies of anything that interests you; accept, as far as text material is concerned, but ask if you can borrow catalogues so that half-tone illustrations may be photographed. Nowadays the quality of photocopying of black and white line drawings and typography is excellent. There is no machine in general use, however, for half-tone reproductions that can match the quality of a copy photograph made by an experienced person.

While you have charge of borrowed material it is your responsibility to look after it with the greatest care, to ensure that your photographer and printer treat it with equal attention and respect, and to see that it is returned as soon as possible after processing – undamaged, properly packed and protected. In certain cases it would be advisable to insure rare items while they are in your possession. Old photographs, in particular, if they are originals, may have a high value. The larger libraries and museums with photographic departments carry out copy work as part of their normal service. The photographs from the Jackson Collection used in this book were made from the original negatives by the University of Glasgow's Photographic section.

---

29 *To our eyes, perhaps, this 1930 kitchen interior, with up-to-date gas cooker and solid-fuel water boiler, is rather austere.*

To finish our exemplary tale, the distant museum had nothing suitable in the way of contemporary photographs, but offered modern photographs from its own records of 1930s light-fittings in period room-settings. Eventually you used two of these. Family and friends produced nothing. Nevertheless, they were all alerted to your interest in old photographs. Much good material is destroyed simply because people are not aware of its potential historical interest and value.

A possibly unique record of the growth of a once-important motor vehicle manufacturer is part of the Albion Archive in Biggar, in southern Scotland. Fig. 31 shows a typical spread from one of the albums there. On left-hand pages – and with commendable brevity – the development of the Albion Motor Car Company is recorded year by year, from its establishment in December 1899 onwards. In 1900, for example, there were two sole partners; the workshop area totalled 3600 square feet (334 sq. m); one 8hp chassis was produced and by the end of that year there were two office staff and five in the 'works'. In 1902 there were three board members, 43 employees in the works and five in the office; paid-up capital at 31 December was £8362 in Ordinary and £650 in Preference shares, and 33 8hp and two 10hp chassis were built.

On right-hand pages four carefully selected photographs appear, showing vehicles, engine or chassis details, works extensions and so on. In full these well-arranged and well-preserved albums provide an extremely interesting and valuable outline history of a firm once important in the British motor industry. They are backed-up by a most comprehensive library of handbooks, sales literature, bound volumes of company magazines, minutes of directors' meetings, press cuttings and an extensive collection of photographs.

To begin and to maintain a record of this sort is easy enough as long as the company concerned, the number of its products and the range of its activities stay at a modest level. By 1920 Albion had 1150 works and 310 staff employees; paid-up capital had risen to £502,862 and production to 1506 vehicles. Nevertheless, it was still a comparatively small concern, with only two or three basic products.

---

30 (opposite) *The electric cooker at an early stage in its development, 1913. Its practical advantages – efficiency, quietness, lack of smoke – were offset by the necessity for daily maintenance.*

---

31 (below) *Each director of the Albion Company received a copy of the album of which two pages are pictured here, covering the period from 1899 to 1900 in the manner shown.*

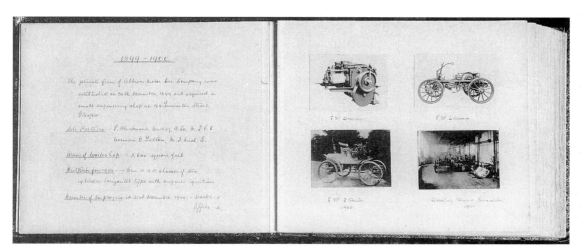

To make a comparable record of a major manufacturing company such as Boots would be a very different affair. Yet many mail-order companies produce enormous illustrated catalogues on an annual basis, the cost of which is justified by their effectiveness as selling agents. In this respect, the history, however good in itself, cannot compete.

There are a few collections by individual photographers which constitute major archival sources in themselves. One of these is the collection of W. F. Jackson, already referred to. In the only reference to him in print seen so far, the railway historian, John Thomas, notes that he was an 'incredible martinet' and a 'fastidious gentleman' – facts which might also be deduced from photographs of this smallish, preoccupied, unsmiling and unusually well-dressed man. Clearly, he took an active interest in clothes, revealed in the number of pictures of the girls and women in his close circle of relatives and friends. Apart from the fact that these are far above the average in terms of clarity and sharpness, many have real pictorial authority as well. A characteristic group of four may be seen in Figs. 32–5.

For technical reasons (large-format cameras, slow films and slow lenses chief among them) early photographers worked outdoors whenever they could. Jackson was no exception and what he could do when conditions were perfect is seen in the extremely well-arranged and well-lit group of family and friends taken in 1909 (Fig. 36). Occasionally, he took his apparatus indoors, with some success, as Fig. 37 shows. This is a valuable record, not only of its sitters, but of the furnishings and decoration of the room. The latter is surprisingly free from the clutter of ornaments, heavy drapes and overpowering patterns that might have been expected.

Although John Thomas refers to Jackson's energy and ability, he makes no mention of his ceaseless travels between 1900 and 1914, when the war reduced their frequency and range. All the year round he and his attendant trio of wife and two nieces were away, either in England and Scotland or abroad, and while he could

have been in London on business it is unlikely that matters of importance to the railways took him to Bournemouth, Broadstairs or Tunbridge Wells.

His photograph of Broadstairs (Fig. 38) is not pictorially exciting and was never intended to be so; it is, however, a first-rate record of a part of the seafront, taken before noon, when people were still moving out of their hotels and boarding houses to the beach or the town centre. There is no wheeled traffic on the road before the terraced houses, only some pedestrians, while others relax on wooden seats. There is a lift to take people to and from the sandy beach below high chalk cliffs, and beside it a remarkably modern-looking flight of stairs. No one seems to have taken to the sea from the regimented rows of wheeled bathing boxes on the right of the picture, and the donkeys close-by are not yet on the move. A substantial number of deck-chairs are occupied, however, and some of Wilson's tents have been hired. Hats, a good deal of dark clothing and a general feeling of formality are notable features of the holidaymakers scattered across the beach. The neat kiosk on the left, occupied by W. Hemstead, Pastrycooks and Confectioners, has no customers yet but there are a few outside the Teas kiosk inshore from the donkeys.

Jackson's Tunbridge Wells photograph (Fig. 39) is every bit as informative, and even more evocative of the time of year at which it was taken. Pedestrians of all ages are warmly dressed, which suggests that the morning was still chilly. One motor car (with a vertically-striped body) is visible, and outside the station on the left six cabs wait for custom. What looks very much like a hotel bus has taken on a party of guests and their trunks – a forerunner of the 'courtesy cars' or buses we know today. The location of the railway station was identified

---

32–5 *Four portraits taken in the garden of 'Glenyon', Gullane, in June and July 1911.* (opposite) *Mrs John Jackson;* (overleaf) *Miss Nellie McGill, the housemaid; Mrs W. F. Jackson; Mr W. F. Jackson*

36 (below) *Although this photograph concentrates on feminine finery, it indicates that building had not yet begun behind 'Glenyon'.*

37 (left above) *W. F. Jackson chose his moment with great care on June 12, 1911, taking full advantage of sunshine outside that was well diffused inside but sufficiently bright to allow a brief exposure.*

38 (left below) *The choice of viewpoint is good for this photograph of the seafront at Broadstairs, taken on June 15, 1912.*

39 (below) *Mount Pleasant, Tunbridge Wells. A first-class example of W. F. Jackson's sensitivity to the quality of light in the early morning.*

from a town plan of Tunbridge in a 1946 RAC Guide (a useful source still to be found at small cost in jumble sales or secondhand bookshops).

Equally atmospheric and informative is Jackson's photograph of a crowded scene in Berwick-upon-Tweed (Fig. 40) with a crowd of street-sweepers clearing up after the horses, a chauffeur-driven Wolseley and many shoppers on the right. The little roofed structure to the left of the car is a mobile office of a municipal kind still to be seen many years afterwards. Another attractive photograph is that of Westminster Abbey (Fig. 41), in which Jackson had made effective use of the strong tonal contrast between pedestrians and vehicles and the great building towering above them. During the same visit to London Jackson recorded the male-dominated scene at the

40 *Berwick-Upon-Tweed, September 9, 1911. Obviously, the fall of the afternoon light was the attraction here, but the pictorial and documentary elements are also superbly balanced.*

41 *Only the purist would take exception to the backward tilt in this otherwise excellent view of Westminster Abbey, April 15, 1912.*

42 *Corner of Seacole Lane and Faringdon Street, London, April 1912. Relics of the huge amount of lettering on business premises may still be found.*

corner of Seacoal Lane and Faringdon Street (Fig. 42). One of the City businessmen wears a top hat; most are bowler-hatted and wear long black overcoats – a uniform commonly seen in other cities, and one that endured until comparatively recent times. Note the litter on the road – no new thing, clearly.

It would be interesting to see a picture of this place taken forty or fifty years later. Such comparisons often have real value. Sometimes they show how little things have changed, as in the example in Fig. 44 (p. 54); at others they reveal how completely the past can be eliminated.

One occasion that has a limited life (as a rule) is the exhibition, whether local, national or international. In Fig. 43 we see the Franco-British Exhibition, in London, in 1908, from a set of postcards that is often encountered. Fig. 45 shows it in 1911, when W. F. Jackson photographed its imposing Shepherd's Bush entrance – architectural bravura in an undistinguished setting. The line of nine motor taxi-cabs and the two closed-top tramcars are signs of things to come – but horses are still drawing heavy loads.

The contrast between everyday life and the artificiality of the big exhibition is brought out in Fig. 46, a view across the Thames to the Festival of Britain, the major event of 1951. It is the sort of subject that tends to be overlooked by most photographers, which is a pity. There was a documentary streak in W. F. Jackson,

Palace of Women's Work, Franco-British Exhibition, London, 1908.

VALENTINE'S SERIES COPYRIGHT

43 *The Palace of Women's Work at the Franco-British Exhibition at White City, London, 1908. A first-rate record photograph – sharp, accurately exposed, and taken from a good viewpoint.*

however; he photographed places and things at least as much as people, though it must be said that he usually chose the latter from his own class. Notable exceptions are Figs. 47 and 48, the miners politely stepping onto the road in Prestonpans to let some ladies pass, and the group of fishers cleaning their lines at Cromarty (taken, one suspects, as much for its pictorial as for its documentary value).

Two photographs of people at work are of interest. Fig. 49, taken in July 1911, reveals that men and women worked together at this time on an almost numerically equal basis. In the

picture of the ruins of Elgin Cathedral (Fig. 50) we see how simple scaffolding was neatly assembled but not at all reassuring.

In the group of coachbuilders (about ninety altogether) taken at the St Rollox Works of the L.M.S. Railway Company by an unknown photographer, the prevalence of flat-caps, dungarees or long aprons, and collars and ties is an indication of the clean nature of their work (Fig. 51). No beards are visible, and few moustaches. Coachbuilders in their workshop are also seen in Fig. 52, taken a year or two earlier at the Newport Pagnell premises of Salmons & Sons. They seemed to have little space to work in – a not uncommon state of affairs at that time.

Passing mention has been made of handout photographs. For most of this century they have been an important part of commercial or

44 *West George Street, Glasgow, looking towards St George's Parish Church, February 1913.*

The same scene in July 1987. The only significant change in the period between the two photographs being taken is the erection of the large bank building on the left of the street.

45 (above) *In 1912 the Shepherd's Bush entrance to White City, the site of the 1908 Franco-British Exhibition, was still an imposing, alien, presence.*

46 (below) *From the Embankment various features of the 1951 Festival of Britain stand out: the Festival Hall, the Skylon and the Dome of Discovery. The everyday life of the Thames and the Embankment continues, with pleasure boat booking offices and ice cream stalls.*

47 *Early morning in Prestonpans – on a weekday if the presence of the miners and the coal cart is anything to go by.*

48 (above) *Fishermen and women cleaning fishing lines at Cromarty, September 25, 1912. In this case physical damage to the negative does not spoil a fine photograph.*

49 (below) *On 6 June 1911, men and women were ricking hay at Muirfield Farm in Gullane. Mechanisation in agriculture was still far off at this date.*

50 *Stonemasons at work on the renovation of Elgin Cathedral, September 1914.*

51 (left above) *The staff of the Carriage and Wagon Department at St Rollox Railway Works, 22 February 1926. Because of their headgear, the higher grades of management were known behind their backs as 'the hats'.*

---

52 (left below) *An extremely well photographed workshop interior, c. 1923. These coachbuilders were skilled craftsmen who worked with wood, metal, leather and glass, using few tools and even fewer machines.*

---

53 (below) *An early 'handout' photograph showing a pre-production Austin Seven at Woodstock, near Oxford. The village is strangely empty. Observe the interesting period lamps and the hand pointing the way to Blenheim.*

industrial publicity, distributed to newspapers and appropriate periodicals, the trade press especially, on a free reproduction basis, and with an accompanying press release. They may illustrate a new product, a new process, a new factory or a new managing director, and, generally speaking, they are of good technical quality. Photographs of new cars, television sets, washing-machines, electric shavers, toilet soaps, women's stockings, curtain materials, carpets, typewriters and computers land on the desks of editors and specialist writers daily.

Progress photographs of major building and civil engineering projects may also be useful. These are made, for administrative, technical and legal reasons, as a matter of course. Mention may be made of the relatively high

54 *From the album of a former officer: troops of a highland regiment at ease in Allouagne in northern France, summer 1915. The softer side of war is very rarely recorded in photographs.*

quality of sets made during the construction of the Forth Railway Bridge in the 1880s and '90s. Equally detailed and effective records were made during the building of the Severn and Humber road bridges. Civil engineering firms and builders ought to be on any list of possible sources.

Architects too maintain a photographic record of their work that is not necessarily confined to pictures of the exteriors of their buildings. If their practice has been in existence long enough, their photographic files may be invaluable. Estate agents and surveyors may also be useful. At the start of any project it is worth considering carefully the professions, official bodies – local authorities planning departments, etc. – and trades which might be relevant. Endeavour to find out how many are within reasonable reach and locate the individuals who might be able to help before you make the initial approach. Your local history librarian or curator, the secretary of your Local History Society, and any fellow historians, as well as the secretaries of professional bodies and trade associations may all be able to help.

Finally, the history of the armed forces in an area can often prove a fruitful subject for investigation. If you are planning to write an

55 *This was no summer picnic, however benign the day. The scene is a mixture of the military and the domestic, with the latter predominating perhaps. The trees are still intact – service at Beuvray was not yet active.*

account of the local Territorial Unit or of a famous regiment with its HQ in your area, your first approach could be made with the help of an acquaintance. On the other hand, you might prefer to contact the Adjutant, because his function is so much concerned with day-to-day administration. Each of the Services is extremely proud of its history and keeps records (see Figs. 54 and 55). Indeed, Regimental museums are by no means uncommon, and the Imperial War Museum, in London, with its vast collection covering the activities of all three Services over a very lengthy period, can be consulted as a further source of pictures and information.

As far as the Royal Air Force is concerned, make your first local contact with the Community Relations Officer of the aerodrome that is your potential subject. For more help, you can refer to the RAF Museum at Hendon. In the case of the Royal Navy write in the first place to the Naval Historical Department, Ministry of Defence, Navy, Old Admiralty Building, Whitehall, London. If you know any former airmen, sailors or soldiers – talk to them. It is surprising what they can usually produce in the way of old photographs.

Chapter Three
SEARCHING FOR PHOTOGRAPHS

When embarking upon a project, tell as many people as you possibly can what you are up to, beginning with close family and friends, then gradually expanding the number of contacts over as wide an area as is practical. It helps if you are part of a large family that has lived in the same place for a very long time, and it helps, too, if you work in a reasonably large company, especially if it has a house magazine or newspaper to which you may turn for publicity for your project. As an alternative there is always the office, staff-room or college notice board.

In any case discuss the matter with your colleagues, remembering always that the more clearly and succinctly you do so the stronger your chances of holding their interest. Whenever a suitable opportunity arises talk to those you see regularly – the postman, for instance, pump attendants at your local filling-station, your newsagent, your hairdresser – and don't forget the tradesmen and others who come about your house; the builder, window-cleaner, milkman, coal- or oil-delivery man, meter readers and so on. If you work at school or college, speak to fellow students and staff.

For those who are naturally shy it is far from easy to initiate and to sustain this sort of verbal enquiry, particularly if the response, at first, is not an encouraging one. On occasion, it must be stressed, however, we all put on an act for one reason or another; we deviate from our normal behaviour to some extent to make a point; to press it home gently or emphatically, as the occasion requires, and the fact that in so doing we are able to hide behind a temporary mask makes it easier to talk and to ask questions with confidence.

One thing the local historian will have to do, now and then, is to speak out with authority. If you are too modest or too self-deprecating, you may not be taken quite as seriously as you deserve. Before laying down the law, however, make absolutely sure of your facts as far as they go, for you may discover, too late, that the person to whom you are talking knows more about your subject than you.

In these days of local, as well as national, radio and television your chances of securing air or screen time are good as long as your subject is of sufficient interest. For obvious reasons, general magazine programmes on each medium attract the greatest numbers. It is up to you to decide whether to approach the producer of one such programme or of a more specialised programme watched by far fewer people. Find out the producer of the programme you select and send him or her a brief outline of your project. If it is of sufficient interest, a research assistant will get in touch to find out more about it – and you – before submitting a report to the producer, who usually makes the final decision.

If you are fortunate, go well prepared and make sure that you arrive at the studio about half an hour before you are due to be taped or filmed. Exposure of this kind can be very rewarding. This writer has spoken on radio many times in connection with specific projects and even while he has been doing so listeners have been 'phoning in with offers of information and photographs. Such is the immediacy of this medium – and television is at least as effective.

Another useful 'shop window' is your local newspaper. In the first place write to the features editor, outlining your project and detailing your photographic requirements. He or she will decide whether to pass your letter over to the appropriate individual for inclusion in the letters page or hand it over to the diarist or columnist responsible for the regular, general interest, gossip feature. You may be surprised

56 *After letters asking for photographs of pre-First World War flyers in Scotland had been published in several local and national newspapers, numerous replies were received. These contemporary postcards of two better-known airmen are typical of the material sent.*

at the response of readers. If you consider that your subject is of sufficient interest and importance, write to your nearest newspaper with a large and wide-reaching circulation – the *Yorkshire Post*, for instance, the *Irish Times*, the *Scotsman*, the *Western Mail*, the *Oban Times*, or even *The Times* itself. There may also be specialist magazines that deal with your subject, such as *The Railway Magazine*, *The Field*, *Country Life*, *Aeroplane Monthly*, *Architects' Journal* or *The British Journal of Photography*. Before you write make certain that those you choose have a letters page, however.

From long experience one learns that the periodical aimed deliberately and successfully at a particular kind of readership can attract a quite remarkable degree of loyalty, and a quick response from those who buy it. A case in point is *The Scots Magazine*, for which this writer prepared a two-part article on what was then known as the Lind Collection of photographs, some years ago. At the time nothing was known about the photographer responsible, who might have been a Cameron, a Jackson, a Readdie or a Snodgrass, these being the names most frequently encountered in the captions with which each picture was furnished. One possible clue to his identity was the number of railway subjects; another was the frequency with which ministers of the United Free Church, their families, their churches and their manses, had been photographed. Was the person responsible a cleric, perhaps, with an interest in railways, whose official duties required much travel in Scotland, along with a certain amount in England and abroad?

The first article appeared in January 1980 and before the end of that month a good deal of information had been sent in by readers. In successive months more was to follow, from many parts of the world. William Fulton Jackson was identified as the photographer; the incidence of so many railway subjects was readily explained by his position as General Manager of the important North British Railway Company, and the presence of so many with a religious content a consequence of his own active involvement in church affairs. One

relative even remembered that Jackson arranged special rail transport for Sunday School outings.

In this instance, the identity of the photographer was established in less than a month. Commonly, however, it takes a great deal longer – if, indeed, it is ever discovered. As we have already seen, identification of photographer as well as of subject is one of the greatest problems encountered when collecting material from private sources. Who is it? What is it? Where is it? When was it? Who took it? To find answers to one, let alone all, of these basic questions is almost impossible. The captioned photograph, whatever its period, is a great rarity, and it is possible to make good use of it in practice.

Let us take two family groups as an example. Between the first (Fig. 57), with father, mother and seven girls and boys, photographed with subtle skill in the Old Cross Studio, Hamilton, in Scotland, and the second (Fig. 58), with grandmother and an assortment of relatives, taken outside a substantial stone-built house in nearby Lanark, the difference in social standing is only obvious after close study. Those seen out of doors are better dressed and more relaxed, whereas the family indoors, in the artificial setting of the studio, are less affluent (some of their clothing has a home-made look). Nevertheless they face the photographer in an alert and confident manner. Photographs of this kind and quality could be used to convey the idea of the large family, of fecundity, as an important social factor at the time of their taking (in all probability the late 1890s); alternatively they might be used to emphasise the formality of dress and deportment in their day.

---

57 (right above) *This is an excellent group photograph – well arranged and day-lit, impressing the viewer with a strong sense of the personalities of the subjects.*

---

58 (right below) *Although the exposure time here may have run to one second, there is no sign of movement – even by the slightly hostile children. Period formality is of the relaxed kind in this case.*

59 *The visual and social significance of the hat was still considerable when this wedding party faced a photographer who knew his business. The grouping is masterful.*

Period flavour is especially strong in the carefully arranged wedding group of 1910 or 1911 (Fig. 59), taken after the ceremony and before bride and groom left for their honeymoon. Utterly different are the groups of Glasgow children, of 1917 and 1928 respectively, shown in Figs. 60 and 61. In the earlier photograph the background is a typical, traditional stone tenement and what we are looking at is a section of the generation that was to become actively involved in the Second World War. In the later picture the background is a recently-built corporation property. Some of the boys might have served as models for

William and his gang of outlaws had they come from a higher social level, and the dress of the girls and the cut of their hair, where visible, closely follows contemporary adult fashion. This is seen, in a somewhat different setting, in Fig. 62, a 1928 photograph of a social occasion in Perthshire. It was the first time round for the short skirt, incidentally; the very beginning of a cyclical process that continues.

Again this is the kind of picture that is

60 (right above) *These Glasgow children have responded well to the photographer but have preserved their independence. Dress is casual and only one child is barefoot.*

61 (right below) *Little adults. One wonders if the girls had borrowed their mothers' hats for the occasion. Most of the boys are wearing boots – a sign of winter, perhaps.*

62 *Cloche hats, shiny silk stockings that had a brief life, smart shoes, smiles all round – the Gay Twenties personified.*

effective in scene setting, giving pictorial flavour to an account of a specific period. Other early photographs are less easy to date accurately. The wearing of the shawl was commonplace in many parts of Britain before the Second World War; by 1945, however, it had become an increasingly rare sight, even in Glasgow, where for centuries it had been worn by working-class women of all ages. In 1948, when Fig. 63 was photographed, were it not for the cars, which are post-war, and the avail-

ability of cauliflowers at 6d (2½p) each, according to a chalked notice outside a greengrocers, the scene depicted might have been taken ten or twenty years earlier.

Care must always be taken in dating old photographs. This is particularly so when dealing with family albums, the contents of which often lack any kind of adequate identification of subject and date. Try to find an elderly relative or friend who has a good and accurate memory – but be ready to cross-check whenever you have the faintest of doubts. If, by chance, the family bible has survived, and if it was used for regular, systematic recording of marriages, births and deaths, you have a generally reliable source of information.

It is never wise to be too dogmatic about dates whenever there is a question of fact. Always qualify in such cases; apart from anything else it proves that you are aware of your responsibilities as a recorder and interpreter of fact.

Before you start to look through unofficial sources make certain that you know what you are after. This you cannot do unless you have a clear and positive view of your subject, of how you propose to deal with it, verbally and pictorially, of how many words and pictures you can use (determined, largely, by the amount of money available for production and by the time required for research).

Unless you are 'self-publishing' (which is not yet quite so easy nor quite as inexpensive as we are told) others will be involved, especially on the financial side, and unless you are unusually fortunate, the budget for photographs is unlikely to be generous. As a result, the fewest possible number of illustrations is going to have to serve with the greatest effect, so you must try to find the very best you can and that is never easy. This is not helped by the fact that you may be compelled to look to unofficial sources, with all the extra time and effort necessarily involved in dealing with largely unclassified and un-identified material. A significant factor, of course, is the matter of reproduction fees, which are less likely to be asked for by private sources.

Flexibility of approach is an advantage. Stick to your predetermined idea of what is essential, but be prepared to consider the unexpected as and when it turns up. Another photograph, taken at a different time of day, might give more information about Birmingham Town Hall than Fig. 64. It is unlikely that it would give such a feeling of excitement, however, of visual drama caused entirely by the fall of light on a particular place, at a particular time of day. It is the sort of scene that only the opportunist photographer with the vision to recognise its pictorial worth at once and with the technical means to record it on film is going to take. W. F. Jackson possessed both attributes, and in spite of the considerable drawbacks of a 1907 camera he caught many such memorable scenes. Another example of his rare ability to 'see' a photograph and to take it when the light was right is the early morning shot of men and women on their way to work, passing the Abbey Court House at Holyrood Palace, in Edinburgh (Fig. 65). The pictorial quality of this fine photograph is matched by its tonal subtlety. Wherever you are looking for photographs be on the alert for ones like these, whatever their subject matter. They can be of people as well as of places, as in the well posed photograph of the Radcliffe Football team (Fig. 66). A high viewpoint adds to the interest of Fig. 67, the unveiling of a war memorial in Langholm, in the Scottish borders, by the Earl Haig. Such a scene was common enough in the 1920s but this is the only photograph of such an occasion this author has come across in postcard form. It was found in a family album.

63 *A once familiar street scene. The shawled old woman and her follower were probably taking rags to a nearby street market.*

64 *In few cities is it possible to walk across the courtyard of a palace – in this case the Palace of Holyrood, Edinburgh, April 1912.*

Let us suppose that you are working on a study, of reasonable length, of your own home town. You have already located a good selection of photographs of the place, which has several public and private buildings of architectural distinction, a couple of large industrial concerns, a brewery and bakery, and a navigable river. Its railway has gone; there is no station and the lines have been removed. In the past, a historically-minded local photographer, with a good head for heights, scaled the tallest church tower and made a series of views all round, and more recently someone followed his example, producing a set of up-to-date pictures to form an interesting and valuable comparison with the previous set. You are still short of pictures of the people of the town, at work and at leisure, the one and only local newspaper having cleared out its photograph library during a waste-paper drive just after the last war. Because its local history section has not been properly established as yet your library cannot help at this stage. It is thus a matter of exploring the

65 *The original is a Judge's postcard dating from the very early 1900s. This is certainly an above average pictorial view of the city, taken in early morning light.*

66 *An expert on football might be able to date this photograph from the length of the players' shorts. These Ratcliffe players were almost certainly pictured pre-1914.*

67 *The Earl Haig unveiling a war memorial at Langholm, in the Scottish borders, 1919. An event of importance to the town, unobtrusively photographed in a way that emphasises a sense of community.*

unofficial sector, beginning at home with family photographs and slowly expanding this activity to include the collections of relatives and friends.

Ask if anyone took a camera to school events of importance – to prize givings, to concerts or plays or pageants, end-of-term exhibitions or sports days. Perhaps a distant cousin was a frequent winner of the sack-race. You make enquiries that confirm the rumours, get in touch, and borrow the one and only picture that has survived. Another relative was perhaps the best player in the town's football team – so good in fact, that he was lured away to a first-division club and became well-known nationally. His proud father assembled a special album of press-cuttings, old programmes and photographs which, mercifully, has survived in excellent condition (see Fig. 68). You may be allowed to use what you want and, afterwards,

you might suggest that the album is presented to your library's local history section.

If you live in an English town it is likely that there is at least one cricket team, in which, over the years, one or more members of your family may have played. Photographs may have survived, but if you cannot locate any within the family get in touch with the club secretary. If the club has been successful over a long period there should be a pictorial record of past triumphs, perhaps even a combined trophies room and museum. Obviously this could apply to other successful sports clubs. Apart from photographs of players, individually and in teams, and of officials, board members or sponsors, look for pictures of the ground itself and of matches in progress.

Before the spread of near-universal motor car ownership, large-scale outings to the country or seaside were extremely popular features of everyday life (see Fig. 71). Some of those who participated took along a Box Brownie or simple folding camera. Pageants, street festivals, processions, marches or walks, open-air markets, visiting fairs and circuses were among the public events that took place, mainly in summertime, all over the country. They were

68 *Probably taken around the turn of the century, this photograph of an unknown team is typical of its time and kind. Essentially serious and informative, it presents pride of achievement.*

69 (above) *The Orion Football Club, Aberdeen, 1902. The arrangement here is less formal than in the previous example, and there is no cup to display. Notice the assortment of headgear, the confident soldier, and the watch-chains.*

70 (below) *A likely source of photographs of cricket teams is school magazines, in which the names of the players are often given.*

well supported, as were such generally popular annual occasions as the agricultural and the flower show (Fig. 72). The former was held out in the open but the latter was housed (as it still is) in a suitable public hall or in a number of marquees. The annual allotments show provided variety.

Before the Second World War, membership of the Boy Scouts, Girl Guides and other youth organisations was widespread and numerically larger than it is now. In Scotland, particularly, the Boys' Brigade had a strong following. Members of these three organisations often attended summer camps, where the use of cameras was encouraged. One feature of Boys' Brigade activities was the weekly church parade, largely an open-air affair, like the

71 *Before the motor car the horse-drawn brake was a popular carrier of those committed to a day out. Here, two three-horse, 14-passenger brakes set out from the Derbyshire town of Glossop.*

regular public performances by Salvation Army bands all over the country.

Until recent times, the Church everywhere, whatever its denomination, was an exceptionally important centre of social activities for many people. Because of its intimate contact with vital aspects of everyday life – weddings, births, christenings and death, for example – it is a basic source of information for the local historian. Apart from the written records which must be referred to on occasion there is the chiselled history on almost every gravestone, tomb or mausoleum. Burial grounds are an extremely important source of information on a variety of subjects and, to some extent, the appearance of gravestones, tombs and mausoleums reflects changing attitudes, not only to design but to death itself. Figs. 73–5 show something of the variety to be discovered in places seldom visited as much as they ought to be.

Pictorial evidence of Church activities is more likely to be found among parishioners than in the church itself. But try there anyway;

72 *Sunday School flower festival, Ireleth with Askam, 1907.*

speak to the minister or preacher, priest or rabbi or vicar, and if a parish magazine or any other kind of periodical exists ask if you may have a little space to refer to your quest for pictures.

For numerous reasons (one of which is the technical challenge offered to the photographer) the recording of church or cathedral interiors has always been of special interest to members of camera clubs or societies (see Fig. 76). Your usual diplomatic approach to the appropriate secretary should lead to contacts with individual members, whose portfolios might include subjects relevant to your project, and from whom it is reasonable to assume willing co-operation.

Portraiture has also been popular with camera club members for a very long time and because of this it is worth asking if any have photographed local personages in the past – important people in the Council or Corporation, for instance, prominent professional persons, businessmen, industrialists, educationists, clerics and so on. Almost certainly, some will have photographed your local town's amateur dramatic or opera society productions during rehearsals, along with portraits of individual actors and singers – the latter either on stage, in costume, or at the club's studio. It was an arrangement suiting all concerned, for the societies received sets of prints that could be used in front-of-house publicity, at little or no cost; the players received prints that they could show off to relatives and friends (and, if they were ambitious, to casting directors), and the

73 *This tombstone at Stanhope, County Durham, was erected over the bodies of Ann and Michael Walton, born in 1676 and 1690 respectively. Its message is conveyed with great simplicity and dignity.*

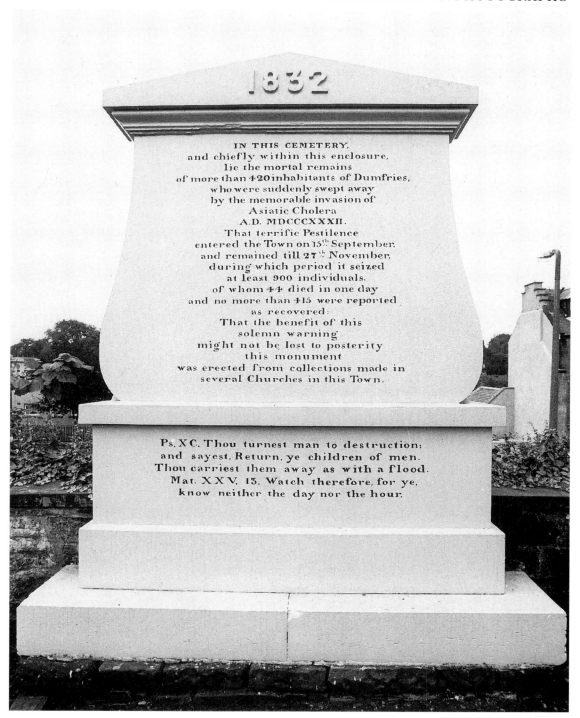

1832

IN THIS CEMETERY,
and chiefly within this enclosure,
lie the mortal remains
of more than 420 inhabitants of Dumfries,
who were suddenly swept away
by the memorable invasion of
Asiatic Cholera
A.D. MDCCCXXXII.
That terrific Pestilence
entered the Town on 15th September,
and remained till 27th November,
during which period it seized
at least 900 individuals,
of whom 44 died in one day
and no more than 415 were reported
as recovered:
That the benefit of this
solemn warning
might not be lost to posterity
this monument
was erected from collections made in
several Churches in this Town.

Ps. XC. Thou turnest man to destruction:
and sayest, Return, ye children of men.
Thou carriest them away as with a flood.
Mat. XXV. 13. Watch therefore, for ye
know neither the day nor the hour.

74 *St Michael's churchyard, Dumfries. Social history is to be found aplenty on tombstones. This one records 'the memorable invasion of Asiatic Cholera . . . that terrific Pestilence' in 1832.*

This Stone
is erected by
CHRISTIAN WEST,
in memory of her
Beloved Husband
GEORGE WATT,
Seaman in B⁺ Macduff;
one of the five who lost their
lives coming from the Fishing
the 16ᵗʰ Decʳ 1802, in the 26ᵗʰ
year of his age.
Also their Daughter
ISABELL WATT, who died
4ᵗʰ June 1802, aged 4 years.
Also the above named
CHRISTIAN WEST
who died 1ˢᵗ Janʳʸ 1859,
aged 93 years.

photographers had the willing services of co-operative models.

If societies of this kind still exist in your area contact their secretaries to ask if there is an archive of photographs of past productions (some taken, no doubt, under the arrangement referred to above; others taken by a professional photographer or by the town's own newspaper). Find out, too, which, if any, of your family and friends had theatrical or musical connections, and what pictorial records they may have. Performers, of course, have seldom shunned the camera or resisted the temptation to show off photographs of themselves.

---

75 (left) *Natural disasters of various kinds are recorded on tombstones throughout the land. The lettering of this one, in northern Scotland, is of superb quality.*

---

76 (below) *A well-taken cathedral interior of the kind favoured by the more able amateur photographer. The date is unknown, but the building, of course, is timeless.*

Choirs of various kinds have always played an extremely important part in the life of many communities; so, too, have brass-bands, with a concentration of interest in each form of musical expression in the industrial areas of the north of England, in south Wales and in central Scotland. In the latter country, of course, the bagpipe-band is still popular. It is possible that members of your own family may have been involved with one or other of these, and that pictures of individual performers, bands and choirs, either posed or in action, at rehearsal, in concert or village hall, or in full performance, perhaps competing at an important festival, survive in private hands.

Dancing, another popular leisure pursuit, enjoyed a strong following over the years, learned, up to a certain level, at day school, with further tuition for the dedicated at local specialist schools. Again, begin at home, then ask friends, and find out if any of the long-established 'dancing academies' have survived.

If they have, make contact with the proprietrix or whoever is now in charge.

We have considered a few spare-time pursuits, but not all; clearly you will make up your own list at an early stage of a project. On the whole, the chances of tracing suitable material are good, as long as you are prepared to spend much time (and persuasion) locating picture hoards. When it comes to finding photographs of people at work, however, you may find things less easy. In the past, as at present, the majority of camera owners tended to use them only in summer, in good weather, and their main subjects were family, friends and pets. Those whose interest in photography was more serious were inclined to join camera clubs

---

77 (left) *Miss Winifred Rumbelow appeared in an advertisement in the 1920 edition of* The British Journal Photographic Almanac. *This is the sort of photograph to look out for in family albums.*

---

78 (below) *The cast of* Tally Ho *at a Liverpool theatre. Further details would require a good deal of research. Because of technical limitations it was necessary to pose such photographs, until the miniature camera came into more general use.*

and to specialise in landscape, architecture or serious portraiture. Record and documentary photography were not highly regarded; indeed they were scorned for their alleged lack of any aesthetic content by some; by others they were dismissed because it was felt that they were too easy.

To a large extent, therefore, work was something that many camera club members did not care to photograph. If they did, they romanticised it as best they could. Occasionally a friend or fellow club member was persuaded

to dress up and make-up as a chimneysweep or a fisherman (complete with sou'-wester, of course) and pose under carefully contrived lighting in a studio setting. Only occasionally would a real joiner, tinsmith, machinist, needlewoman or artist be photographed at work, and this sort of picture is particularly worth looking out for.

To be fair to those concerned, early photographers had difficult technical problems to cope with until they all overcame their great distrust of the 35mm camera after the last war. The equipment they favoured was often unwieldy, and viewfinder systems, except on the bulky single-lens reflex cameras much used by press photographers, were inefficient and slow in use. Fast lenses were not commonly seen, although they were available, and fast emulsions were quite unknown. As a result, unless the light was exceptionally bright it was necessary to secure the camera to as substantial

79 W. F. Jackson's photographs were un-manipulated, but many amateurs of his day tried out various processes designed to emulate the effect of the painter. One such process, Bromoil, relied upon the application of pigment to the print, and was used with above average skill by J. C. Warburg to romanticise this view of asphalters in London, c. 1923.

a tripod as it was possible to carry and to give an exposure of some length (see Fig. 80). Just how long depended on circumstances – but it could run to whole seconds instead of fractions thereof. This was of no great matter as long as the subject was a static one but it could cause problems in portrait photography if the sitter was required to 'freeze' for a perceptible length of time. Yet so great was the skill of many operators in this specialised field that their portraits have a remarkably spontaneous air.

Another problem facing the user of the large-format camera was that of securing an adequate depth of focus in photographs, especially those taken at fairly close quarters. This could be overcome by using a 'field' or similar type which had a range of mechanical movements allowing great control of the depth of sharpness available. The size, weight and slowness in action of apparatus of this sort made it unsuitable for everyday snapshot work, however, and the box- or folding-cameras that used

80 *Interior of a late nineteenth-century studio. Daylight was a favoured source of illumination, its intensity carefully controlled by blinds and screens of varying opacity.*

81 *A typical folding, roll-film camera, from a 1912 Boots catalogue. The fact that the viewfinder was at waist level explains the low viewpoint of so many old photographs.*

roll-film and became increasingly popular after their general introduction at the beginning of this century were much more convenient (see Fig. 81).

Although W. F. Jackson was an accomplished technician he took few satisfactory photographs indoors. The examples in his collection lacked sharpness, either because of camera movement or because of an insufficient depth of focus at the wide lens apertures he was forced to use. With the proper equipment, of course, complete sharpness of image, from closest foreground to most distant background, is readily obtained, even on the largest available film. The user of the 35mm format and one or

other of the high-quality wide-angle lenses so readily available nowadays knows little or nothing of a problem once almost universal.

Photographs *were* taken of people at work, nevertheless, by both amateurs and professionals, and it may well be that some from each of these sources have survived in domestic collections. On occasion, prints found their way from company files into the hands of employees – years after they were taken, as a rule. The view of the interior of the Bathgate garage of the S.M.T. Company (Fig. 82) was made in 1929 and it came into the possession of the writer in 1951 when, as Art Editor of the *S.M.T. Magazine*, he was clearing non-topical material from its library. Another photograph from the same source (and of about the same date) is Fig. 83, showing a 'road metal crushing Depot' in the Sma' Glen, in Perthshire. Apart from the crusher itself, with its attendant cloud of dust, two steam road-rollers, a steam-waggon, two

---

82 *Bus depot, Bathgate, c. 1929. Notice the printed destination bills stuck to the bus windows, and the leggings worn by drivers and conductors as part of their uniform.*

83 *Roadmending at Sma' Glen, Perthshire, c. 1929.*

tar-boilers and a pair of living-caravans, plus three workmen, can be seen. The little house is still there. It is generally safe to assume that it will be much easier to find outdoor pictures of this kind than useable ones of people at work indoors.

Once you have investigated the private sources known to you, make an approach to the important industrial concerns in your town, as well as the brewery and bakery, smaller businesses like builders, plumbers, tailors and so on, and shopkeepers.

The importance of the shop in social life is of very long standing and the rate of change in its appearance was relatively slow until quite recent times. While there is some chance of tracing privately taken pictures of members of staff posed, rather self-consciously, outside their place of work, it is suggested that a more reliable source would be your library or local museum. Where a shop has survived, unchanged, for a lengthy period, try the present owner. The very fact that he has not altered it in any significant way indicates a strong personal interest, pride even, in its appearance. If nothing of any age is available it is, of course, permissible to use a modern photograph. Some examples of the quality and documentary interest of the well-preserved shop-front are shown in Figs. 84–6.

It should be mentioned here that if a

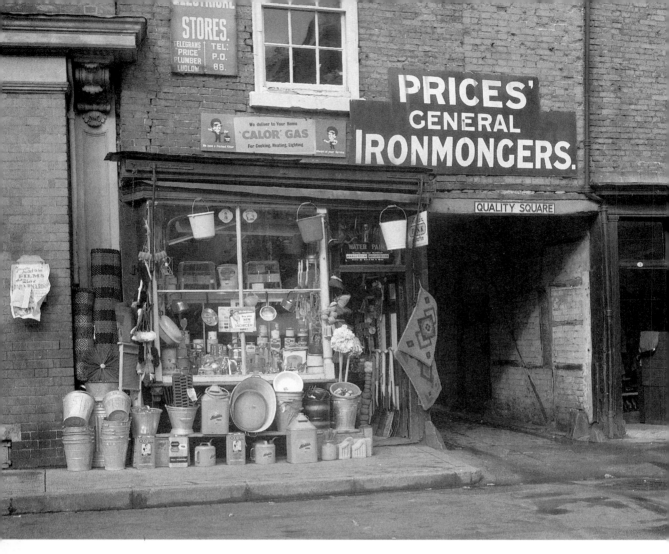

newsagent's shop is visible in a street scene, and if the newspaper placards are legible, it is often possible to date the picture with reasonable, or absolute, accuracy. Posters, whether fixed to walls, gables, special hoardings or to the sides of buses or trams, provide another means of establishing the time of taking. In undated interiors – as long as they are sufficiently sharp – look for wall or desk calendars. In W. F. Jackson's portrait of John Seth on duty at Gullane Railway Station, taken on 19 August 1914, a newspaper bill on the bookstall to his right reads 'France Welcomed Kilted Regiments', and above the smartly dressed boys a magazine cover carries a Prussian-looking face (Fig. 87).

84 (above) *Ludlow, Shropshire, 1958. Traditionally – and for good practical reasons, given its size – the ironmonger's stock is placed outside the shop.*

85 (right above) *Tradition preserved at Jermyn Street, London, where in 1983 this Edwardian-looking butcher's shop was a reminder of past standards of quality in design.*

86 (right below) *Cullen's corner store in Ebury Street, Victoria, London, 1958. Black and gilt were here used to great effect in the external design.*

88

87 *The stationmaster at Gullane, August 1914.*

88 *A recently launched submarine, c. 1915, built by Scott's of Greenock, on trial in the Clyde estuary. One of a number of highly unofficial photographs found in a family album.*

The two pictures (Figs. 88 and 89) of a submarine in the Firth of Clyde during the First World War, and of shipyard and naval personnel in attendance, were inherited by the daughter of one of those present, a submarine engine specialist. She also acquired her father's notebook, containing details of all the vessels built by his employers, Scotts' Shipbuilding & Engineering Co. Ltd., of Greenock, during his time of employment there. In spite of this it has not been found possible to identify the submarine, the only clue being the word 'Dolphin' on the cap of the rating on the right, in the group portrait (Fig. 89).

This writer remembers seeing something similar at the Rover Car Company's Solihull factory during the 1960s when he was researching a history of the firm. It was a pocket notebook carried by the then works manager during the 1920s, containing details of every single product, with brief specifications and costings – not of any direct value as a guide to photographs but an excellent source of information all the same.

When it comes to man-made objects, makers' catalogues and publicity material can help – as long as one can find them. Specialist annuals like *The British Journal Photographic Almanac* or *The Army & Navy Stores Catalogue* carry an enormous number of facts, figures, illustrations and advertisements. Year after year, before the Second World War, small boys and grown men

89 *A group of naval personnel and shipyard officials break from their duties for a formal portrait.*

alike pored over the catalogues of the model train and railway manufacturers – firms as famous as Basset Lowke, of Northampton, or Meccano, of Liverpool (responsible for the enormously popular Hornby trains). Toy catalogues were also published each year by the most important toy retailers in London, those best remembered carrying the names of Hamleys and Gamages.

Reference works such as these are now extremely scarce and fetch high prices on the rare occasions when copies come up for sale. Ask round your family and friends, just in case any have survived, then try your local library and museum. Find out if there are any model railway enthusiasts in your town – and any serious toy collectors; if you draw blanks there then write to one or other of the fine toy museums for help. Remember that they are likely to have collections of photographs as well. In recent years, the number of periodicals dealing with toys and models of every imaginable kind has increased greatly. Many have correspondence pages and it is worth writing to the ones covering your particular subject if you require further material.

A possible subject for a historian living in or near Northampton could be the activities of Bassett Lowke there, which began in 1899, and continued until after the Second World War, and those of Mettoy Ltd., which lasted from 1934 until 1984. In each case a considerable number of former employees are still alive and active in their town, so it is not yet too late to find facts and, perhaps, photographs as well. Nowadays, because of the much greater interest taken by the press and the public in most things of the past – even the comparatively recent past

– there is a better chance of material surviving. One must act swiftly, however, if one hears of factories, businesses or shops about to close down for good. Apart from yourself, libraries and museums will be taking note and so, too, will the dealers. This is a main reason for the great rise in the price of old photographs. If you are a habitual visitor to markets, antique fairs, Oxfam shops, jumble sales and car-boot sales, then watch for albums or loose copies of photographs – you might be lucky.

Chapter Four

SELECTION AND PROCESSING FOR REPRODUCTION

Reference has already been made to the importance of looking at as many photographs as is possible, practically speaking, and of learning how to distinguish the good from the average. It is easy enough to reject those that are in really poor condition – so faded on the one hand, so dark on the other that their image is scarcely discernible and certainly unfit for reproduction, or too badly damaged, physically, to be of any real value. If nothing better can be found, of course, it may be necessary to use material of inferior quality – but only as a last resort.

A further problem concerns the one and only existing picture of a person, place, event or thing. The only available photograph will also be already familiar. Where there is no known alternative it is up to you to decide whether or not to use pictures in this category. It depends greatly on how important the visual complement is, in relation to your text, and in the end this is the deciding factor. In most cases, however, the chances of having to resolve a problem of this kind are unlikely.

The probability of finding material of local interest is greatest in your own area, as long as there are suitable sources, public and private. Look elsewhere, as a matter of course; over the years people move, take their possessions with them, and eventually these find their way into the appropriate sale-rooms or auctions, and thence to antique and junk shops, secondhand booksellers and market stalls. Because of the great increase in interest in old photographs during the past ten years or so the number on offer has increased; so, unfortunately, has their price. Only too often this has scant relation to the quality of material available; too many willing, but completely unselective, buyers

have been seduced by the sight of sepia prints.

In spite of the considerable rise in prices it is still possible to buy advantageously. The writer has found that secondhand bookshops in places off main tourist routes are an excellent source of reasonably priced prints – loose ones in particular. It has to be remembered that many people nowadays buy old photograph albums for display purposes only and take little or no interest in their contents. In much the same way, old cameras are purchased, not for use, but for domestic show. The inevitable consequence has been a steady increase in cost.

So, beware when buying. Look warily at photographs and albums in the antique fairs that seem to be held everywhere these days and pay more attention to the displays of postcards. Even when these are arranged by subject it takes a long, long time to go through them, one by one, yet, tedious as this can be, it is worth doing. To find the larger viewcard that was turned out in such great quantities last century by George Washington Wilson, by the firms of Valentine, Judge and Frith and others, is uncommon. Quite recently, however, the writer was delighted to find a box of cards of this kind in a secondhand booksellers, in excellent condition, in great variety and reasonably priced. One point to remember if one is startled at the cost of old photographs is that this is almost certain to be below that demanded by a picture library for the right to reproduce a picture once only. As long as it is out of copyright – at present this is fifty years after the death of the original holder (although changes to Copyright Law are imminent at the time of writing) – you are free to use it as you wish.

The accompanying photograph of the library of Hatfield House (Fig. 90) was one of those

90 *The library of Hatfield House, Hertfordshire, the seat of the Cecil family, built by Robert, Earl of Salisbury.*

discovered by this writer, bought undated but thought to have been taken in the 1890s along with the pictorially striking street scene in Dumfries (Fig. 91). The impact of photographs of such a dramatic kind can be used to very good effect, either to draw attention to the publication in which it appears (preferably as a cover illustration) or as a means of enhancing the look of a page inside. Be careful, however, that it does not dominate; a photograph with such 'punch' can be reproduced quite small yet retain its special power.

The matter of design, including layout, is most unlikely to be the direct concern of the local historian, but it can help to select pictures capable of being reproduced in a variety of shapes, this applying in particular to photo-

graphs taken outdoors. It will give the designer more scope if, for example, he has beside him upright as well as horizontal views of a specific subject. For obvious reasons most portraits take the upright shape unless they are close-ups, in which case it may well be possible to trim them to an almost square format; group portraits almost always assume the horizontal, or 'landscape' shape.

The direction in which a subject is looking is also worth considering; as a general rule it is better if he or she looks into the centre of the book and not outwards.

You will gain the gratitude of your designer if you are able to supply variety of choice here as well. This is a matter taken into account by any good library when making-up a selection of photographs to send out on approval. As far as is possible the prints should also have a tonal match: they should not range from the very light to the very dark. If they do, for

95

91 *High Street, Dumfries, towards the end of the last century. This is a street scene of high quality, with the clock tower in the distance as a focal point of interest.*

unavoidable reasons, ensure that they do not appear on the same page spread.

The single-subject photograph can stand much more reduction than the one offering a great deal of information. The impact of the former is little diminished when reproduced at a small scale. The exceptional amount of detailed information in the view of central Bristol (Fig. 92), on the other hand, would be largely lost were it to be reduced too much. A 'stamp head' portrait reproduction is one thing: a stamp size landscape quite another.

Mention has already been made of the importance of securing photographs that are as sharp as possible and have as wide a range of tone as good printmaking can provide, even

when it is known that they are going to be reproduced at a modest size. It is as well to have, as it were, a great reserve in these important respects, for at some future date a large-scale reproduction may be required – as a magazine illustration, perhaps, or as a photographic poster, or as an all-enveloping cover illustration. The unsharp print, the one that is either too contrasty or too flat, is of no use in such cases unless it has some special pictorial value that can be usefully exploited by great enlargement.

Unsharpness was sought after at one time by both amateurs and professionals and brought about by various techniques. The 'edge' of a picture could be taken off by unscrewing the front element of the lens a trifle, by attaching a diffusing-screen before it or by using a specially computed 'soft-focus' lens. It was a technique practised with superb skill by Hollywood still photographers during the 1920s and part of the '30s and used, when appropriate, by their movie-making contemporaries. The average amateur could not really compete, having neither the technical skills nor the resources of the professionals. If you do come across photographs of the soft-focus sort judge them on their merits, pictorially speaking, and on their actual value as documentary evidence.

An interesting practical application of photography is revealed in Fig. 93, a small advertising card for an Isle of Wight hotel; found, incidentally, along with others of the same sort, among the viewcards mentioned above. Even to the naked eye it is obvious that much retouching was carried out on the original plate or negative, probably because it lacked clarity of detail, sufficient tonal contrast and enough people. Although the photographer's name appears on the left, the name W. Gray appears on the stone wall on the extreme right of the little print. Was he the retoucher responsible for so much of the picture?

Since the beginnings of motoring in this country, in the 1890s, it has been customary to photograph new cars outside their suppliers' premises or in the process of being handed over

---

92 *A summer afternoon in Bristol, c. 1928, looking towards the floating harbour and the tramways centre from Broad Quay. Surprisingly, open top tramcars were still in use in Bristol at this time.*

NICHOLSON. PHOTO.   20, MILL STREET, VENTNOR.

Banchurch Hotel, Banchurch, Ventnor,

SLE OF WIGHT.   H. RIBBANDS, PROPRIETOR.

93 (above) *This enlarged print of a tiny original (c. 1875) has not been cleaned up for reproduction – quite deliberately.*

94 (below) *Kilmarnock, c. 1908. Many motor dealers at this time had started off in the cycle business, in the boom years towards the end of the last century, and had held on to this trade as a useful sideline.*

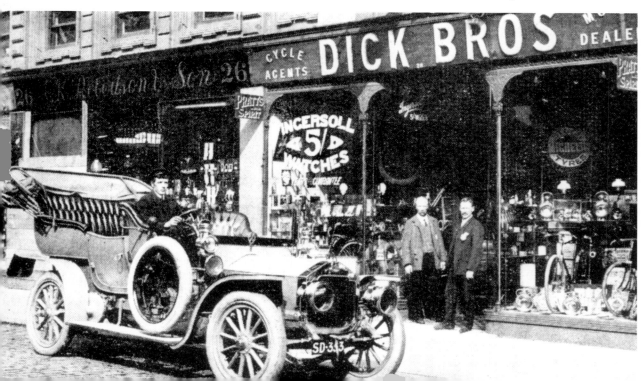

95 *A Leyland-Crossley bus, 1905. Only the passengers inside on the lower deck had any protection in this kind of vehicle. Mechanical reliability was generally poor. Convenience and novelty were the main attractions, however.*

to their new (and still smiling) owners, with publicity as a prime concern. Fig. 94 shows a new Albion touring car posed outside the showroom of Dick Brothers, along with the proprietors. The photograph was copied from a small half-tone reproduction in a tartan-bound history of the firm, and because this operation was carried out with great attention to accuracy of focus and exposure, and final printing made with equal care, it is close to the original in sharpness and tonal range. A good copy-negative of this sort of subject can be enlarged to a considerable degree (thereby revealing much additional information) although as the degree of magnification increases the half-tone dot becomes more and more visible. The photograph of the open-top bus (Fig. 95) was also copied from a reproduction, in this case a fairly large magazine advertisement.

At the time when the totally untypical Glasgow pawn-shop was recorded (Fig. 96) it occupied the stump of a tenement in a cleared area of the East-end. The lettering, with its mixture of hard but humorous selling and information, is its main interest; its whole appearance unique in a city that once had more than its share of traditionally dark and reticent

96 *Glasgow, c. 1960. This photograph of a pawnshop is self-explanatory.*

pawnbroking establishments. But here, for quite a short time, a little bit of social history was writ large. Entirely different is the exterior of the Glasgow optician's shop in Fig. 97, with its overall simplicity, elegance of proportion and subtlety of detail. The shop was opened in 1896 by John Quinton Pringle, who was not only highly skilled in his craft as optician and instrument maker and repairer but was a spare-time painter of rare sensitivity and quality whose reputation has grown steadily. He occupied these premises (which he also used as a studio) until his retirement in 1923. Note the unusual, almost surreal, pair of eyes serving as shop sign.

The Fox & Hounds Inn, at Barley, in Hertfordshire, flies its sign across the road in the shape of well-drawn fox, hounds and huntsmen on horseback while, beneath, a group of real rustics and the driver of the little car respond to the photographer (Fig. 98). The postcard of Marykirk (Fig. 99), which is subtly tinted in the original, is around twenty years older; clouds have been added to the glass negative and lines strengthened to some extent in the houses in the middle distance, but this work has been well done and the viewpoint chosen is a good one.

97 *A unique shopfront which disappeared in the modernisation of Saltmarket, Glasgow, some years ago.*

98 (above) *Barley, Hertfordshire, c. 1924. Very typical of its time, the period feel of this photograph is emphasised by the telegraph poles and the predominance of thatched roofs.*

99 (below) *Marykirk, c. 1905. Three forms of transport are caught together at a time when the motor car was still an uncommon sight in Northern Scotland.*

100 *Summer in the western highlands, c. 1929. The motor ferry at Ballachulish takes on passengers.*

From the 1920s hikers, of both sexes, became an ever more numerous sight in Britain, sturdily dressed and shod in what at times amounted to a quite distinctive uniform. A photograph would not be out of place in any study of an area popular with walkers in pre-war days. Fig. 100 shows a group of locals, flappers and hikers gossiping at Ballachulish Ferry, in the West Highlands. With photographs of this quality there is nothing to worry about; they are very good of their kind and they will reproduce well on almost any kind of paper.

The view of Cults House in Aberdeen (Fig. 101) is in fair condition, apart from a long white scratch on the right that could be touched-out quite easily. It lacks contrast, however. This could be restored to something of its original vigour by careful copying and equally careful printing. The house itself is of sufficient historical interest to justify such attention and, unlike this photograph, it has not faded away.

We have already discussed photographs that lack any positive dating features – the kind once so popular with the publishers of postcards and viewcards. Fig. 102 is an example from the late 1950s that might have been taken ten or twenty

101 (above) *Cults House, Aberdeen. Although there is no evidence as to when this photograph was taken, the clothing of the man and the children beyond suggests a date in the early 1870s.*

102 (below) *Glazed glass of contrasting colours, elaborate woodwork and stained and etched glass are typical period features of licensed premises built before the Second World War.*

103 *St Andrews, 1929. HRH The Duke of York* (left) *with Andra Kirkcaldy, a famous golfer of his day. By close trimming, interest is concentrated on the most important part of the photograph.*

104 *Although Miss Reid is more appropriately dressed for afternoon tea than for sport, her fine appearance made its intended effect on the croquet lawn.*

105 *Race day at Kelso, in the Scottish borders, soon after the end of the First World War. Only the poorly proportioned, classically inclined main grandstand remains today.*

years earlier. It shows an Oxford public-house exterior. Take away the ventilator on the right of the door and, perhaps, the word 'Halls' (with its post-war look) and it would be very hard to say whether it had been taken before the war or after.

We have also taken a passing look at the difficulties of dating from clothes and have decided that in most cases it is best to hand over the problems for solution by the specialist. Occasionally, the evidence is strong enough to allow a reasonably accurate estimate to be made, a good example being the newspaper photograph of the then Duke of York, later King George VI, at his installation as Captain of the Royal and Ancient Golf Club at St Andrews (Fig. 103). During most of the 1920s and much of the '30s 'plus-fours' were popular, especially

with golfers – as may be learned from any good history of costume. As it happens, the original print (found in a jumble sale) bears the date 26 September 1929 on its back. It is reproduced here with the art department's 'crop-marks' left in to show how trimming was indicated to the block- or plate-maker.

For comparison, examine W. F. Jackson's portrait of 'Miss Reid, croquetting at Shalimar, Strathaven'. She is wearing normal dress. It will be noticed that in each of these sporting studies there is a lot of unnecessary background on either side. For reproduction it could be trimmed to the extent necessary. By intelligent cropping, attention can be concentrated wherever one requires it. Alternatively unwanted detail may be stopped out, either on the negative (as long as it is large enough) or on the print itself, but in either case this is a task for someone of great skill and experience. In the photography of machine-tools, for example, it is often necessary to take them in the factory where they are made, with all the attendant untidiness and relative uncleanliness that this implies. Sable-brushing or air-brushing must come later.

In the original print of the racecourse scene (Fig. 105) there is an excessive amount of sky. For reproduction here it has been reduced to a considerable degree but the foreground has not been touched. The picture itself is interesting, with the rows of rather down-at-heel motor-cars, the unfashionably dressed racegoers and the makeshift-looking grandstand. In the album from which it was taken there was a photograph of an obviously prosperous spectator offering his large cigar-case to a friend – the sort of once-common, everyday happening that was so seldom recorded. The print was much too faint to copy successfully, however.

Where racing has long been an important element in the daily life of a place it might make an excellent subject for study as long as one had sufficient fore-knowledge of the sport. Finding sufficient photographs would not be difficult in view of the average owner's or trainer's interest in maintaining a record of his or her animals, successful or not. One breeder of trotting-horses known to the writer had a complete photographic index of his stable since its foundation in the late 1920s, each subject appearing in the approved stance in the formal records, and in addition he had pictures of races and the presentation of awards.

With so many people actively involved in racing – owners, trainers, breeders, jockeys, stable-boys, specialist photographers, etc. – the range of choice of material should be a wide one. Apart from the horses, look out for good pictures of stables, tack rooms, exercise and training areas, and personnel, not forgetting grooms.

Mention has been made of the 'approved stance' for horses in photographs. There is one right way, and any number of wrong ways, of photographing the horse; rigid rules as far as the placing of legs and hooves, head, ears and mane, and tail are concerned must be followed, which is why the specialist in this subject has to be involved. The same state of affairs applies to other livestock and to certain domestic animals also, and in your researches you will see many

examples. You will also see less formal photographs that may well complement the 'approved' ones on the printed page.

Another potentially rewarding subject could be the use of the horse in agriculture, with specific reference to your own area, and if you happen to live in a district in which hunting and point-to-point events have been a feature of everyday life over a sufficiently long period these activities could be covered also. But before you start, have a word or two with the Secretary of the local Young Farmers' Club, to find out what he or she thinks of your idea. Always consult those with knowledge and some authority, if you can, at the earliest possible stage of any project, for it is likely that they have information about what has been done already (but is not yet in print) or what is still in preparation. They should also know if nothing has been done, in which case you can go ahead unhindered.

An alternative could be an investigation of the use of the horse in urban life. Until it was replaced by the motor vehicle it was the principal source of mobile power on our roads, and on our canals it remained in service in sizeable numbers long after the internal combustion engine had been introduced there. It was in daily use by architects, bakers, butchers, coal merchants, dairymen, drapers, doctors, greengrocers, grocers, hirers, laundry-men, lawyers, newspaper owners, plumbers, post offices, tea and provisions merchants, bus and tramway operators; by undertakers; by Councils, County Councils and Corporations, large or small; by the Army; by the very railway

106 (right above) *Birmingham, c. 1909. This area has changed enormously since the 1900s, and with it the special qualities of the indoor and outdoor markets that were a major attraction at weekends.*

107 (right below) *Great Orme's Head, Llandudno, c. 1924. According to a note on the back of this postcard, the tramcar had 'a Bad Smash in August 1932, 2 killed'. An example of the long commercial life of a postcard.*

High Street and Bull Ring, Birmingham.

TRAMWAY, GT ORME'S HEAD, LLANDUDNO.

108 *Dover Harbour, c. 1910. Afternoon light on a rather untidy and crowded scene. The extended Admiralty Harbour breakwater – just below the horizon on the left – was completed in 1909.*

companies which had so effectively eliminated the horse from long-distance transport of goods and passengers during the nineteenth century, and by the owners of livery stables and riding schools. The scale and scope of this subject are wide-reaching.

In many old photographs, the horse-drawn bus and tram offer the specialist clues for dating. The former, which first appeared in London as early as 1829 and whose active working life continued for 90 years or so, is less often seen than the latter, which did not come into regular and general use until 1870 or thereabouts. It is not difficult to discover when these quite distinctive types entered service in your town or city: ask at your local history library or museum, or consult the vast literature on the subject.

The electric tram was in service in London from the turn of the century until the early 1950s. In Glasgow, the horse-drawn tram appeared in 1874 but by 1900 the electric vehicle had proved itself, and by 1902 had taken over completely. With such elementary knowledge it is not difficult to rough date photographs of street scenes in these or other cities and towns. Problems may still arise, however. The postcard of Birmingham (Fig. 106) is a Valentine production that looks as if it was taken around 1909; here one is relying on the look of two distant motor-cars and the dress of the comparatively small number of women. The presence of a closed-top, double-deck tramcar on the right, however, introduces doubt because of its 1920s look – and because there is so much obvious retouching elsewhere. Such suspicion has to be part of the historian's nature. In fact, examination under a strong glass reveals that the tram has open stair-tops at each end and is thus contemporaneous with the rest of the photograph. Final doubts could be settled by consultation with the staff of the first-class Central Reference Library in Birmingham or of the nearby Museum of Science and Industry.

The important 'chance' element in picture

---

109 *The rectory at Hambledon in Hampshire, with windows open and blinds down in summer.*

research recently operated in this writer's favour: he had acquired an undated viewcard of Llandudno, die-stamped 'Frith's Series' and taken at a time when that Welsh town was substantially built but covered a comparatively small area. Dating it was a task to be tackled only by someone with local knowledge. Within weeks he came across a postcard of Llandudno, postmarked 1933 and taken from almost the same spot – but later – by an unknown photographer (Fig. 107). In the Frith picture, which may have been made in the 1890s, the

110 *The elements of an English village: farm buildings, carts, church, a cottage, a well-built brick wall and a neat wooden fence. The village is Hambledon, Hampshire.*

road down from Great Orme's Head is bare. In the second, shown here, there are tram rails and drainage channels and the distant town has grown noticeably in size. When so much has happened during a given period it is exciting to find visual evidence of such a kind.

About the port of Dover the present writer knows little, which makes dating the postcard shown in Fig. 108 difficult. There are one or two clues, however: scarcely a sailing vessel to be seen, numerous paddle-steamers that could be identified with relative ease, and the harbour itself. As it happens, there is a reference to extensions to the Admiralty Harbour between 1898 and 1909, as well as a small map, in *Engineering For Boys*, by Ellison Hawkes (an early editor of *The Meccano Magazine*, incidentally), which supports one's deduction about approximate date – but a final cry for help would have to go to Dover.

It would prove less easy to discover from Hambledon, in Hampshire, just when the photographs of the village shown in Figs. 109 and 110 were made. The original prints are sepia-toned, quite sharp and of good quality. They are square, which suggests that they may have been taken with a 6 × 6 cm camera – quite possibly a Rolleiflex, the popularity of which grew during the 1930s. The only real evidence of age is the presence of two fine farm carts in one of the pictures. They are of a type that was out of general use long before the last war. They

are unusually clean for vehicles in daily agricultural work. There are no wheel tracks visible on the grass around or beneath them; it is summer, however, and, perhaps, there had been a long spell of dry weather. The only possible way of finding out would be to visit Hambledon itself and make a door-to-door enquiry – which might be totally impractical.

Yet photographs of this kind and quality are just the sort that one would hope to find for a projected history of such a village. It has close and widely well-known associations with the earliest days of cricket in England, and pride of place would have to be given to subjects like Broadpenny Down, for example, where the game was played during the eighteenth century; to the Memorial to the Hambledon Cricket Club that faces the Bat and Ball Inn; to the Inn itself, inside and out, along with any interesting

111 *By careful trimming and much skilled retouching this photograph could be made quite suitable for reproduction.*

mementoes of cricket that might be on view, and to any other items or places of historical importance. One would not overlook the village church and school, of course. Perhaps the Bat and Ball might serve as the most suitable place for initial enquiries.

Unfortunately, not all the photographs that we acquire are in such good condition as these; yet, because they show things of great importance to us we are sometimes compelled to use them. By the look of Fig. 111, the picture had been carried around in its owner's pocket for years before he decided to get rid of it. Nevertheless the most important area of the photograph – that occupied by the players – is good enough for satisfactory reproduction. If necessary, a certain amount of salvage work could be carried out – but only by a retoucher of considerable skill and practical experience.

In practice it is quite difficult to decide when to retouch and when to leave alone, the latter course being the one that it is tempting to follow when the imperfections actually emphasise the age of the print. As long as any blemishes do not interfere with the clarity of the image overall there is much to be said for leaving them as they are.

When you first examine old newspaper photographs you may be greatly surprised at the crudeness of their retouching, especially in the case of sports pictures that were processed at high speed (more often than not the prints were made from still-wet negatives) and retouched with equal haste, to make them suitable for reproduction on poor quality newsprint. At close quarters this work seems rough and ready; remember, though, that it was essential during a period when plate or film emulsions and camera lenses were very much slower than their latter-day equivalents. The sports photographer trying to capture action on a football or rugby pitch in January afternoon gloom, with a large-format press- or reflex-camera (a 5 in. × 4 in. negative was commonly used), a slow lens (with extremely limited depth of sharp focus at the wide apertures usually necessary) and emulsions of restricted speed and latitude, needed all the help he could muster, once his negatives

reached the darkroom. Nowadays, with 35mm cameras, extra-fast lenses and films of a sensitivity only dreamed of less than twenty years ago, his successors have a much easier time.

Nevertheless, the users of those bulky press cameras turned out work of remarkable quality whenever circumstances were in their favour. Those who tended to produce sports photographs of exceptional merit usually had the good fortune to work in summertime – covering cricket, for instance, or yacht racing. One remembers striking telephoto shots of cricket, taken from outside the ground on occasion because a rival had managed to secure exclusive rights to photograph the game, and the timeless pictures of racing yachts and almost every other kind of sailing vessel made from 1881 until the present day by Beken, of Cowes, the most widely-known of the specialists in this field. Until comparatively recent times their preferred cameras were specially made and of the box pattern, but instead of roll-film, as in the universally popular Brownie, these cameras used $8\frac{1}{2}$ in × $6\frac{1}{2}$ (22cm × 16cm) glass plates, and were hand-held in a fast-moving motorboat. Another specialist of comparable excellence was Charles E. Brown, whose photographs of aeroplanes in flight are also remembered for their superb quality. His work was to be seen regularly, over a lengthy period, in the leading aeronautical publications.

As part of anyone's personal photographic education it is worth spending time studying the work of specialists of this calibre. Since the great increase in interest in old photographs began a decade or so ago, a growing number of books and monographs on individual photographers has appeared, many of which are available in the larger libraries (see also Bibliography, p. 123). Some years ago the work of the Abrahams brothers was commemorated in book form. Over a lengthy period they recorded their home territory, the English Lake District, comprehensively and with great competence. Their work was sold to publishers and, from their premises in Keswick, to the public, postcards and original prints being the mainstay of their business.

In Scotland outstanding landscape photographs were taken by Robert M. Adam during the first fifty years or so of this century and much used by publishers fully aware of their special qualities. An English contemporary of comparable stature was Frank C. Smythe, who had a reputation as mountaineer, photographer and writer that was richly deserved. For his very fine Alpine and Himalayan pictures he used an Etui, a lightweight roll-film camera. Adam, on the other hand, travelled the length and breadth of Scotland with equipment that weighed around 50 lbs. These exceptional men played no tricks with their medium, and never resorted to the manipulations favoured by so many contemporaries.

Another artist who chose to use photography as his medium was Frank Sutcliffe, whose photographs of Whitby and its surroundings set standards of pictorial excellence and documentary thoroughness that will stand for all time. Indeed it is doubtful if a better record of the look and life of an English town over an extended period has ever been made. In spite of the fact that he used an $8\frac{1}{2}$ in $\times$ $6\frac{1}{2}$ in (22 cm $\times$ 16cm) hand-and-stand camera, mounted on a tripod, Sutcliffe was able, time and time again, to take spontaneous-looking pictures of the fisherfolk and other inhabitants of Whitby. In Glasgow the firm of T. & R. Annan & Sons produced photographs of the city, made between the 1890s and the 1930s, of above-average quality.

Look out too for the industrial photographs taken before and after the last war by Walter Nurnberg and Harold White, whose work had great style and impact. Also, the picture stories – many featuring manufacturing processes of various sorts – made by J. Allan Cash, an all-rounder, must be remembered for their fine pictorial quality and their exceptional suitability for reproduction. It was a pleasure to receive a batch of prints from Cash; there was always at least one striking 'lead' picture that could be used on the first page of the relevant article to attract attention, along with a mixture of horizontal and upright shots to satisfy both art editor and designer. This photographer's ability to tell a story in pictures, with the minimum of words necessary to explain them, was of a special kind. In picture journalism of the type most effectively represented in *Picture Post* the work of Bert Hardy was seldom bettered. He too was a master of the picture story; moreover he had a special ability to relax sitters, who began by being suspicious but soon loosened up in his reassuring presence. His contribution to social history in this country is an important one.

The above examples are a sample only, of a personal nature; it is by no means comprehensive yet it will introduce you to some of the best work of its kind produced in Britain since the last century. Any time spent on examination of photographs of acknowledged excellence is never time wasted; consciously or not, you will gain from it in the long run. Any sharpening of one's critical faculties will make it easier to decide what, and what not, to use to illustrate one's own work.

Local and national newspapers may, from time to time, use old photographs that may be of direct interest. As far as the nationals are concerned take a critical look, now and again; try to determine what it is about this picture or that that compels your attention and interest and, subsequently, use such findings to help you select the best from what is available for any given project.

During the second half of the 1930s *The Times* published numerous fine pictures, its unnamed photographers making most effective use of filters in landscape work, and pioneering the use of infra-red film for selected subjects. Until the 1950s many of the 'quality' newspapers made a regular feature of non-news photographs, especially at weekends, and the practice may have stopped, gradually, as growing affluence enabled more and more of their readers to go hither and thither to see places for themselves. Perhaps, however, it was a simple matter of changing fashion.

Since the last war, certain newspapers have paid particular attention to the standard of photographs reproduced, among them the *Observer*, the *Guardian*, the *Financial Times*, the *Sunday Times* and, most recently, the *Independent*. The latter has been publishing photographs of quite exceptional quality since it first appeared in 1986 (laying up a store of marvellous material for the local historian of the future as it does so). Often its news pictures have pictorial value as well.

So far nothing has been said about exhibitions of photographs, the number and frequency of which have grown steadily during the past twenty years or so. At one time the annual exhibition of the local camera club was the most that could be expected. Nowadays, however, the chances of seeing the work of individuals or of groups, not simply on a local but on a national and even an international scale are very good; furthermore, standards of presentation have risen, along with the quality of printed matter, either in catalogue or full-length book form. Photography is now taken more seriously than ever before.

Although it is to be hoped that your selected pictures will tell their own story, it will be necessary to provide them with captions, the length and nature of which will vary from one subject to another. At times the baldest of descriptions is sufficient; at others it will be essential to draw attention to visual features that require explanation. Fig. 1 is an example of this. One would not like to claim that caption-writing is an art but it is certainly something that comes more easily to some people than others and, as with so many other things, it tends to improve greatly with experience. Once more, draw on commonsense as a guide; avoid saying the obvious if you possibly can! To caption a straightforward picture of a cow with the words 'A cow' is not quite enough; tell your reader what kind of cow it is and what it has achieved in the way of high milk yield, record output of calves or successes in competition. Supporting facts of this sort are valuable in themselves, and if you can provide material additional to the text, the caption will acquire greater interest.

Chapter Five

PHOTOGRAPHIC TECHNIQUES FOR THE LOCAL HISTORIAN

Although the matter of the local historian taking an active part in photography has not been discussed in any detail, it has been suggested that from a long-term point of view there is a good case for recording nowadays what is likely to be of historical interest and value in the future. The problem, of course, is knowing which subjects should be photographed. Whether or not you do become involved is very much a matter of personal inclination and economic circumstances. If you intend to carry out a sustained and substantial amount of photographic work there is much to be said for becoming your own cameraman, in terms of convenience and economy.

In general, photography is a relatively easy affair nowadays. The chances of success, in terms of sharpness of image and correctness of exposure, are high; almost everything, it seems, has been done by designers and manufacturers to make their equipment foolproof, with automatic control of exposure, focusing and winding-on, easy loading and unloading, built-in flash that requires no complicated calculations, and overall ease of handling. The only thing beyond their powers to date is the holding steady of the camera itself – one of the two largest causes of unsharp pictures. Properly understood and properly used, the modern camera can produce impressive results; if, however, it is handled carelessly – and its very ease of use encourages this – it will not.

For visual note-taking, as it were, modern 35mm compacts are extremely useful. The fact that most of these ingenious little machines have a semi-wide angle lens is a decided advantage most of the time, and it is only when close-up work is contemplated that a practical shortcoming becomes apparent. There is a limit to how near the compact may be taken to its subject, ranging from 18 in. (45cm) to 39 in. (1m), and while special close-up attachments are available, they are neither very easy nor very convenient to use.

For most kinds of photography, and for working at close quarters in particular, by far the most versatile camera is a single-lens reflex, using 35mm film and fitted with a 50mm lens – one that allows focusing to 15 in. (38cm) or less, at which distance an area around $8\frac{1}{2}$ in. $\times$ $5\frac{1}{2}$ in. (22cm $\times$ 14cm) is covered. With the aid of special close-up (or supplementary) lenses that screw into the front of the camera lens, or of extension-tubes that separate the latter from the camera body, it is possible to make much closer approaches to the subject, so that objects or documents may be recorded, in whole or in part, at any required degree of reduction.

But for the best results, for the ultimate in sharpness and a total lack of optical distortion, the ideal lens is one of the 'macro' type, the focusing range of which normally extends from infinity to a few centimetres. At its closest, the subject is recorded at half its actual size, and with a single extension-tube or ring the image on film appears at same size. Apart from the superb quality of the image that it produces the 'macro' excels in ease and convenience of use. Unfortunately they are expensive, even second-hand; while a good example, from Canon Nikon or Pentax, for instance, would cost nearly double bought new. But for many – the majority, perhaps – the reassurance of guarantees in the latter case is a powerful deciding factor. This writer has bought most of his cameras in used condition and has had almost no trouble at all with breakdowns – but he does know what to look for, and he buys only from sources he knows to be absolutely trustworthy.

Whatever you decide to do, seek as much

informed advice as you can find; consult really knowledgeable friends, colleagues, tutors, photographic technicians and, if you possibly can, a local professional who is aware of your special needs, interested in your projects and willing to help from a strictly practical point of view. And do track down that most potentially useful and helpful of individuals, the camera dealer who has retained his initial interest in the equipment that he sells; who knows the pros and cons of the apparatus that he handles and will advise as to the suitability of this camera, the unsuitability of that, for the kind of photography that you intended to practise. Keep away from the chain-store dealer selling cameras along with TV sets, video recorders and all manner of electrical goods.

What follows is suggested as being suitable for all reasonable photographic needs, and most of the items listed may be bought secondhand if necessary:

(a) A 35mm single-lens reflex camera, with an f1.8 or f2, 50mm lens. A lens of higher speed – an f1.4, for example – will cost much more and give inferior results at close range. Make sure that the shutter has a delayed action and speeds down to 1 second, or longer.

(b) A set of 3 close-up lenses or a set of 3 extension-tubes – the latter of the automatic kind if you can afford them.

(c) Three filters – a blue, a yellow and an orange.

(d) A small spirit-level.

(e) A Kodak 'Grey Card'.

(f) Several sheets of black paper, of various sizes.

(g) A copying-stand and/or a sturdy tripod and a music-stand.

(h) A pair of adjustable table-lamps.

(i) Elastic bands of many sizes, narrow white tape, 'Blu-tack', large-diameter drawing-pins, plain pins, several small round magnets and a sizeable piece of black velvet.

For those who lack practical experience of close-up work and of copying such things as old photographs, documents, pages of books and so on, a brief explanation of the function and importance of some of the items listed above will help.

The spirit-level is necessary to ensure that camera and flat copy are square, one to the other. The 'Grey Card' is essential for the determination of correct exposure for black and white subject matter – pages of books and periodicals, line drawings and diagrams and small half-tone reproductions. In most of these there will be a predominance of white, which gives a misleading reading on your exposure-meter (it will suggest the correct exposure for the white area alone). By placing the card (which is of uniform tone overall) on top of your copy and taking a reading from it you will arrive at the correct exposure for the page. (Before you fire the shutter, make sure that the card is out of the way.) If what you are photographing is tonal – a photograph or a reproduction that fills the viewfinder, for instance – it is permissible to take a direct reading.

With poor quality newsprint or with certain kinds of thin paper you will encounter the problem of 'showthrough', the appearance of printed material on the reverse in faint form. To reduce or entirely eliminate this visual intrusion the sheet of black paper is slipped behind the page to be copied. If you have an old photograph that has a message written across it in blue ink that you want to eliminate place a blue filter over the camera lens and photograph through it. If, on the other hand, you have faded blue ink writing to copy do so through a yellow or orange filter, with an exposure increase of from two to four times, according to the density of filter used. Photographs that have faded to yellow may be copied through a blue filter and detail scarcely visible on the original recovered to a remarkable extent.

Copying of this kind has to be carried out with the greatest of care and attention; unless it is, the result will be much inferior to the original. Often one is dealing with prints from an album, full of detail and sharp – but far too small for use. Only by careful copying may their factual potential be properly realised.

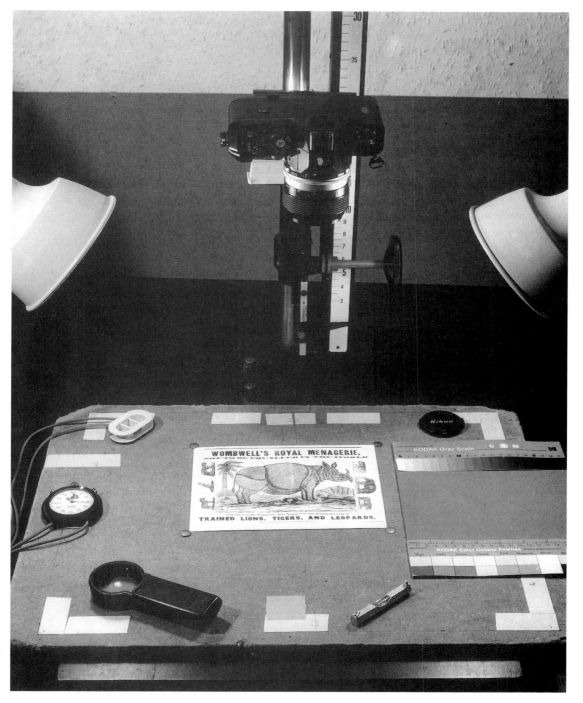

112 *A typical copying set-up: camera mounted on copy-stand, with film-plane parallel to the base-board, an adjustable table-lamp on either side, at 45° to the material being photographed, a Kodak Gray Card and a stop-watch (for time exposures, when necessary).*

Fig. 112 shows one of the copying set-ups used by the writer. For studio work a pre-war enlarger, converted into a vertical copy-stand at small cost, is preferred; it is extremely rigid and the rack-and-pinion drive of the camera, up and down the tall column, saves time and effort. The base-board is covered with a close-textured cork sheet, into which large headed drawing-pins are pushed to hold down the copy material, as shown, without physical penetration. If the copy is expendable, plain pins are used. Another method of holding material flat is to use small magnets as corner pieces, with an enlarger masking-frame of metal as a support.

If you have to copy a photograph that is below glass, problems can arise from reflection of the camera, its operator and his surrounds. One method of eliminating reflection is to make a cut-out for the lens in a very large piece of black card – large enough to conceal camera and tripod. As long as the camera has a delayed-action mechanism you can set that in motion, retire from the scene and wait until the shutter has been fired. The alternative is to drape black cloth over everything that might reflect, then operate the delayed-action lever.

The trickiest of all forms of copying is the photographing of pages or specific items in tightly bound books. Here, one must rely on elastic bands or carefully tied tapes to coax the page into some degree of flatness.

The music-stand, along with a really substantial tripod, is much used by the writer on assignments away from his studio. The material to be copied is secured to the metal top of the stand by magnets, unless it is either too thick or too large, in which case a sheet of polystyrene or plaster-board is used as support. The whole is set at an angle to the vertical, sufficient to keep it in place, and the camera's back made parallel to the copy.

By now, you may be convinced that it would be a much better idea to find a collaborator to carry out the photographic side of your projects. He or she might be a fellow local historian or a member of a camera club. To work with others is no bad thing, as a rule; with each party concentrating on something that he or she knows about and can do well, there is every chance that standards of quality overall will be raised. How you arrange financial matters is a matter for discussion at the earliest possible stage. If you are fortunate, it may be possible to do this on the basis of your assuming responsibility for the provision of materials and the settling of processing charges and other essential costs of travel and telephone calls, for example. At a later date, if work is published at a profit, an agreed percentage might go to the photographer concerned.

It is essential that anyone working with you is a competent photographer, but you must also find out how reliable prospective collaborators are likely to be; how ready and able they are to produce pictures to order, and to do so, perhaps, at short notice. You have to be certain, too, that they are prepared to accept the fact that while their services will be fully acknowledged, whatever the nature of your shared project, the prospects for eventual monetary reward are not going to be great.

Reference has been made to the possibility of making a profit from a publication, now and then. Although it would be unwise to assume that this will occur as a matter of course, it is as well to be prepared to deal with a surplus, should it materialise. Some of those concerned choose to plough back their profits, to help finance future projects. (This is the policy of Joy Monteith, the Chief Librarian of Inverclyde District Council, who has been responsible for the publication of a number of first-class and commercially successful collections of old photographs of towns and villages in her area.)

As far as ownership of copyright in any photographs taken for you by a collaborator, or collaborators, is concerned that is another matter to be discussed and settled at the earliest possible moment. Under normal circumstances, copyright in photographs is the property of the person who commissions them, and the professional photographer retains negatives unless he agrees to surrender them, on payment of an agreed additional fee. In your special circumstances, however, the kind of photograph most likely to be taken for you will

113 *A suitable subject for the photocopier: a reproduction of a litho-chalk drawing of W. F. Jackson.*

be a copy, either of an old document or an old photograph, and the chances of it being used again are small. Remember, all the same, to raise the matter and agree a method of dealing with it. And make sure that everyone involved has a note in writing of what has been agreed.

So far we have looked at copying in terms of straightforward photography. But there are other, cheaper and much speedier methods available nowadays, in the shape of accessible and easily-used photocopying machines. They are only really useful when documents or line drawings are to be copied. If photographs, either in the original or in half-tone repro-duction, are the subject the lack of subtlety of the process in rendering tonal gradations correctly is a practical drawback as far as further reproduction is concerned.

Local history budgets being what they are, it is highly unlikely that you will be working with colour photographs. You may find yourself dealing with early colour prints, of course, dating from the early 1950s when these started to become the norm in family albums. To make a satisfactory black and white print from early colour negative stock requires use of a special paper called 'Panalure', made by Kodak. This usually has to be specially ordered. It is neither cheap nor easy to handle, but it does do tonal justice to the negatives. From more recent colour negatives it is possible to make perfectly acceptable black and white prints on normal photographic papers. Perhaps, however, the simplest solution to the problem is to hand the negatives over to your nearest processor and let him get on with it. His costs should be reasonable, his service can be very speedy and the results tend to be excellent. If the negatives are unavailable, good black and white prints may also be made from copy negatives of colour prints.

BIBLIOGRAPHY

The following is a list of books consulted at one stage or another during the preparation of *Photographs and Local History*, and although it may seem somewhat long it is a fair reflection of the breadth of general and specialised background reading necessarily required for such a task. In practice, the local historian ought not to have to refer to such a wide variety of printed sources; local Post Office directories, large-scale maps, guides, newspaper files, photograph collections and the local library and museum will be his or her main sources. To read outside one's own immediate subject is no bad thing, however, nor is looking at as many old pictures as possible, regardless, almost, of subject.

Most of the following categories are self-explanatory, but in certain instances a word or two of explanation may be of help. During the past decade or two the general increase in interest in things of the past has led to the publication of numerous books of old photographs, mostly collected from a variety of sources, but usually covering a specific period, place or subject. Some of these are listed under 'Collections'. Special attention is drawn to the pioneering series from which *Victorian and Edwardian Liverpool and the North-West* has been singled out, and to *Catherine Cookson Country*, which contains an extremely well chosen and well annotated selection of period photographs of quite exceptional quality and relevance. 'Local history' is concerned with source books on the subject, whereas 'Local histories' deals with publications concerned with specific places or occasions. *Old Inverness in Pictures* and *Chryston* (about a small Lanarkshire village, near Glasgow) are singled out as especially good examples of the value of concentration and team-work at the picture-research stage. Both *Bygone Bedford* and *Edwardian Blackpool* also stand out, not least for the impression that each gives of those

responsible having enjoyed themselves.

Finally, attention is drawn to the very high standard of reproduction of the Godfrey edition of out-of-copyright Ordnance Survey maps. Along with the almost impossible to obtain town plans originally supplied with Post Office directories, they are absolutely invaluable sources of information as well as being a delight to the eye.

Collections

BENTLEY, NICOLAS, *Edwardian Album*, Sphere, 1974

CHANDLER, GEORGE, *Victorian and Edwardian Liverpool and the North-West*, B. T. Batsford Ltd, 1972

COOKSON, CATHERINE, *Catherine Cookson Country*, Corgi, 1987

MACDONALD, GUS, *Camera: A Victorian Eyewitness*, B. T. Batsford Ltd, 1979

SANSOM, W. M., *Victorian Life in Photographs*, Thames and Hudson, 1974

WINTER, GORDON, *The Golden Years 1903–1913*, Penguin Books/David & Charles, 1977/1975

WINTER, GORDON, *A Country Camera 1844–1914*, Penguin Books/Country Life, 1973

Costume and dress

GINSBERG, MADELEINE, *Victorian Dress in Photographs*, B. T. Batsford Ltd, 1982

LAVER, JAMES, *Costume and Fashion: A Concise History*, Thames and Hudson, 1969

LANSDELL, AVRIL, *Fashion à la Carte 1860–1900*, Shire Publications, 1985

DE MARLY, DIANA, *Working Dress*, B. T. Batsford Ltd, 1986

Gazetteers and Guides

The Illustrated Road Book of England and Wales, Automobile Association, 1958

Road Book of Scotland, Automobile Association, 1957

Royal Automobile Club Guide & Handbook 1946–1947, Royal Automobile Club, 1946

Broadstairs Guide, Broadstairs and St Peter's Urban District Council, 1953

A Pictorial and Descriptive Guide to London and its Environs, Ward, Lock & Co., 1922

General Reading

BATSFORD, HARRY, *How to See the Country*, B. T. Batsford Ltd, 1940

BRIGGS, ASA, *Victorian Cities*, Penguin, 1975

CLUNN, HAROLD, *The Face of London*, 1932

FORSYTH, ALASTAIR, *Buildings for the Age*, Royal Commission on Historical Monuments, England/HMSO, 1982

MACDONAGH, MICHAEL, *Festivals and Customs: Sir Benjamin Stone's Pictures*, Cassell, 1906

STEEL, DON and TAYLOR, LAWRENCE (eds.), *Family History in Focus*, Lutterworth Press, 1984

WILKES, PETER, *An Illustrated History of Farming*, Spurbooks, 1978

WILLSHER, BETTY, *Understanding Scottish Graveyards*, Chambers, 1985

Industry

HUME, JOHN R. and MOSS, MICHAEL. *Clyde Shipbuilding*, B. T. Batsford Ltd, 1975

HURLEY, JACK (ed.), *Industry and the Photographic Image*, Dover House (USA), 1980

MCCUTCHEON, W. A., *The Industrial Archaeology of Northern Ireland*, Department of the Environment for Northern Ireland/HMSO, 1980

NICHOLSON, MURDOCH and O'NEILL, MARK, *Glasgow: Locomotive Builder to the World*, Polygon Books/Springburn Museum/Glasgow District Libraries, 1987

RAISTRICK, A., *Industrial Archaeology*, Paladin, 1973

Libraries

World Guide to Libraries, K. G. Saur, Munich

Local History

Local Studies Library: A User's Guide, Nottinghamshire County Council Leisure Services/Libraries

MOODY, DAVID, *Scottish Local History: An Introductory Guide*, B. T. Batsford Ltd, 1986

RAVENSDALE, J. R., *History on Your Doorstep*, BBC, 1982

RIDEN, PHILIP, *Local History: A Handbook for Beginners*, B. T. Batsford Ltd, 1983

Local Histories

DUTHIE, BILL, *Chryston: A North Lanarkshire Village*, Strathkelvin District Council/Auld Kirk Museum Publications No. 16, 1987

MACLEAN, LORAINE (ed.), *Old Inverness in Pictures*, Inverness Field Club, 1978

MONTEITH, JOY and ANDERSON, MATT, *Greenock from Old Photographs, Vol. I*, Inverclyde District Libraries, 1980

MARSH, JOHN, *Life in Old Lakeland*, Dalesman Books, 1985

PALMER, G. J. and TURNER, B. R., *Edwardian Blackpool*, 1970

WILDMAN, RICHARD, *Bygone Bedford*

Maps

Old Ordnance Survey Maps: Durham City, 1915, Alan Godfrey

LYNAM, EDWARD, *British Maps and Mapmakers*, Collins, 1944

Museums and Galleries

ALCOCK, SHEILA (ed.), *Museums and Galleries in Great Britain and Ireland*, British Leisure Publications, annual

BAIN, ALICE (ed.), *Scottish Museums and Galleries Guide*, Scottish Museums Council, 1986

Photography: General

GERNSHEIM, HELMUT and ALISON, *A Concise History of Photography*, Thames & Hudson, 1965

Practical Photography

ANGEL, HEATHER, *The Book of Close-up Photography*, Ebury Press, 1983

BUCHANAN, TERRY, *Photographing Historical Buildings*, Royal Commission on Ancient Monuments England/HMSO, 1983

COOTE, JACK, *Monochrome Darkroom Practice*, Focal Press, 1982

FREEMAN, MICHAEL, *The Photographer's Studio Manual*, Collins, 1984

HEDGCOE, JOHN, *The Photographer's Handbook*, Ebury Press, 1977

Individual photographers

ABBOT, BERENICE, *New York in the Thirties*, Dover House (USA), 1973

FEININGER, ANDREAS, *Feininger's Chicago*, Dover House (USA), 1980

FEININGER, ANDREAS, *New York*, Ziff Davis Publishing Co., 1948

HOPKINSON, TOM, *Bert Hardy*, Gordon Fraser, 1975

OLIVER, GEORGE, *Robert Moyes Adam: Photographer 1885–1967*, Scottish Arts Council, 1969

PONTING, HERBERT, *The Great White South*, Duckworth, 1921

SHAW, BILL EGLON, *Frank Meadows Sutcliffe, 1870–1910*, The Sutcliffe Gallery, 1974/1985

Photographic Research and Collections

EAKINS, R., *Picture Sources UK*, Macdonald, 1985

EVANS, HILARY and MARY, *Picture Researcher's Handbook*, Van Nostrand Reinhold, 1986

EVANS, HILARY, *The Art of Picture Research*, David & Charles, 1979

WALL, JOHN, *Directory of British Photographic Collections*, Heinemann, 1977

Picture Postcards

HILL, C. W., *Picture Postcards*, Shire Publications, 1987

LUND, BRIAN, *Postcard Collecting*, Reflections of a Bygone Age, 1985

STAFF, F., *The Picture Postcard and its Origins*, Lutterworth Press, 1966

Topographical

BETJEMAN, JOHN, *Shell Guide: Devon*, Architectural Press, 1938

DOYLE, LYNN, *The Spirit of Ireland*, B. T. Batsford Ltd, 1935

EDWARDS, TUDOR, *The Face of Wales*, B. T. Batsford Ltd, 1950

FORD, CHARLES BRADLEY, *The Landscape of England*, B. T. Batsford Ltd, 1933

FLOYD, MICHAEL, *The Face of Ireland*, B. T. Batsford Ltd, 1937

QUIGLEY, HUGH and ADAM, ROBERT M., *The Highlands of Scotland*, B. T. Batsford Ltd, 1936

Transport

ALLEN GEOFFREY FREEMAN, *An Illustrated History of Railways in Britain*, Marshall Cavendish, 1979

BLAKE, GEORGE, *British Ships and Shipbuilding*, Collins, 1946

BIBLIOGRAPHY

CRAIG, ROBIN, *The Ship: Steam Tramps and Cargo Liners: 1850–1950*, National Maritime Museum/HMSO, 1980

GIBBS SMITH, C. H., *A History of Flying*, B. T. Batsford Ltd, 1953

KLAPPER, CHARLES, *The Golden Age of Tramways*, David & Charles, 1961

NOCK, O. S., *The Railways of Britain, Past and Present*, B. T. Batsford Ltd, 1947

OLIVER, GEORGE, *Cars and Coachbuilding*, Sotheby Parke Bernet/IBCAM, 1981

Canals and Canal Architecture, Shire Publications Ltd

INDEX

(Note: page references in italics refer to illustrations.)

Abbott, Berenice *New York in the 'Thirties* 14
Aberdeen, Cults House 103, *104*
Aberdeen, Orion Football Club *75*
Aberdeen University Library 36
Aberystwyth Public Library 36
Abington Museum 36
Abrahams Brothers, Keswick 114
Adam, Robert Moyes 114
Aerial photographs 36, *37*, 38
Aerial views 36
Aerofilms 36
Aeroplanes 114
Agricultural Show 76
Airmen *65*
Albion 43
Albion album *43*
Allouagne *62*
All-steam procession *27*
Alpine and Himalayan pictures 115
Annan, T. and R. 115
Approved stance for horses 108
Argyll motor cars 9, *9*, 10, 20
Argyll Motors Limited 10
Argylls Limited 10
Army and Navy Stores catalogue 91
Arnold Library, Nottingham 36
Astor family 36
Austin Seven *61*

Ballachulish ferry 103, *103*
Bands, brass and bagpipe 81
Bangor, Northern Ireland 11, *12*
Barley, Herts. 100, *102*
Basset Lowke 92, 93
Bathgate Bus Depot 86, *86*
Beamish Museum 35
Beken of Cowes 114
Berwick-upon-Tweed 49, *50*
Beuvray *63*
Biggar 43
Birmingham Central Library History and Geography Dept 36

Birmingham Central Reference Library 111
Birmingham Museum of Science and Industry 111
Birmingham postcard 109, *109*
Blarney Hotel *33*
Blarney Stone 30
Bournemouth 12, *13*, 44
Boys' Brigade 76
Boy Scouts 76
Bridges: Forth Railway, Humber, Severn 62
Bristol 96, *97*
British Journal Photographic Almanac 91
Broadstairs 44, *48*
Burial grounds 76

Cameras 83, 84, *85*, 86, 112, 114, 117, 118.
Canals 22, *23*, 108
Candid photograph 15
Captions 116
Cash, J. Allan 115
Catalogues 41, 44
Cathedral interior 77, *81*
Central Office of Information 36
Choirs 81
Church 76
Circuses 74
Close-up work 117
Clyde Shipping Co. 27, 29, 30
S.S. Coningbeg 30
Colour photographs 122
Copying 41, 118, *119*, 120, 122
Copyright 94, 120
Cork 27, 30, *31*
Cricket 74, *75*, 113
Cromarty 53, *58*

Dancing 81, *82*
Dating photographs 70
Deck billiards *32*

Differences in dress 10
Documentary films 38
Dover *110*, 112, 113
Dramatic society 77
Duke of York, 1929 *105*, 107
Dumfries, St Michael's graveyard *79*
street scene 95, *96*
Dundee *37*

Earl Haig 71
Edinburgh, Abbey Court House, Holyrood Palace 71, *72*
Niddrie 24
Eire 12
Elgin Cathedral 53, *59*
English Lake District 114
Erick's Entertainers 16, *16*
Exposure 118
Extension-tubes 117, 118

Fairs 74
Family album 9, 17, 70, 82, 122
Family groups 66, *67*
Feininger, Andreas 14
Festival of Britain, 1951 52, *56*
Filters 115, 118
Financial Times 115
Flower festival *72*
Franco-British Exhibition, London, 1908 52, *53*
entrance, 1912 *56*
Frith 35, 38, 94, 111

Gay Twenties 70
Glasgow, Bell Street *9*, 10
children 68, *69*
and Cork 27, *32*
optician's shop 100, *101*
pawnshop 99, *100*
Springburn 24
St Rollox Railway Works *37*, 38, 53, *60*

West George Street *44, 45*
West Nile Street 20, *21*
Glasgow Herald, The 29
Glossop 76
Gravestones 76
Great Orme's Head,
  Llandudno *109*, 112
Group photographs 28, *29*, *36*, 44,
  66, *67*, 68, *68*, *69*
Guardian, The 115
Gullane 15, *15*, 16, *17*, 17, *18*, 47,
  88, *90*
Hambledon *111*, *112*, 113, 114
Handout photograph 53, *61*
Hardy, Bert 115
Hatfield House 94, *95*
Hikers 103
Horses 108
Horse-drawn brake 76
  bus 100
  carriage *22*
  tram 110
  vehicle 20, *20*, 21, *21*, 22

Imperial War Museum 63
Independent, The 116
Industrial photographs 115
Inverclyde District Council 120
Ireland 12
Ironbridge Museum 35

Jackson Collection 7, 41
Jackson, Mrs John *45*
Jackson, Mr W. F. 13, 15, 16, 22,
  24, 27, 44, *47*, 49, 52, 66, 71, 86,
  121
Jackson, Mrs W. F. *47*
Judge 94

Lantern slides 24, 27, 30, 31
Lind, William 6
London, asphalters at work *83*
London trams 110
Ludlow *89*

McGill, Miss Nellie *46*
'Macro' lens 117
Mansell Collection 36
Maps 38, 123
Marches 74
Marykirk 100, *102*
Mettoy Ltd 93
Model railway clubs 24

Moody, David 6
Morris Eight 12
Museums 39
Music stand 118, 120

National Motor Museum 35
National Trust 36
National Trust for Scotland 36
Natural disasters *80*
Newspapers photographs 107
  placards 88
North Berwick 16
North British Locomotive Co. 24
North British Railway Co. 24, 66
Northern Ireland Information
  Service 36

Observer, The 115
Official sources 35
Open-air markets 74
Open-top bus 99, *99*
Open society 77

Parish magazine 77
Paterson, Dr L. 30
Pawek, Dr 34
Period flavour 68
Period look 24
Photocopying 122
Photographer's studio *84*
Picture Post 115
Picture researcher 8
Picture Researcher's Handbook 39
Picture Sources, UK 36, 38
Pierrots' Show 16
Plymouth 24, *26*
Popperfoto 36
Portraiture 77
Postcards 35, 94
Post Office directories 123
Prestonpans 53, *57*
Pringle, J. Q. 100
Processions 74
Progress pictures 61

Racing *107*, 108
RAF 63
Ratcliffe 71, *73*
Record photographs 8, 83
Retouching 114
Richmond showground 22
Roadmending *87*, 88
Rothesay 17, *19*
Royal Navy 63

Salisbury 24, *28*
Salmons and Sons 53, *60*
Salvage work 114
Scots Magazine 6, 30, 66
Scott's of Greenock 91, *91*
Shops, Cullen's Stores, London 89
  Paxton & Whitfield, London *89*
  Price's General Ironmongers,
    Ludlow *88*
Smith, Edwin, Photographs 36
Smythe, Frank 115
Sports days 74
Sports photographs 114
St Andrews 107
Stage photography *82*
Submarine 91, *91*, 92
Sunday school outing 24, 27, *28*, *29*,
  66
Sunday Times 115
Sunnyhurst *34*
Sutcliffe, Frank 115

Thomas, John 44
Times, The 115
Tombstones *78*, *79*, *80*
Toy catalogue 97
Tramcar 110
Transport museums 35
Tuck, Raphael 35
Tunbridge Wells 49, *49*

United Free Church 66
University of Cambridge 38
  of Glasgow 29, *41*
  of Reading 36
University College of North
  Wales 36
Unofficial sources 71

Valentine 35, 94, 110
Victoria and Albert Museum 35
Viewcards 94

Westminster Abbey 50, *51*
Whitby 115
Wight, Isle of 97, *98*
Wilson, George Washington 35, 36,
  94
Windsor 17, *18*
Wordie and Co. 10, *21*
Work 53, 82, *83*, 83, 86, 87
Workshop *52*

Young Farmers' Club 100